# YELLOWSTONE
## NATIONAL PARK TRAVEL GUIDE

*Explore Geysers, Wildlife & Scenic Trails with Maps, Camping Tips & Must-See Spots for the Perfect Adventure in America's First National Park*

NASH CORBIN

# Copyright

All rights reserved. No part of this publication may be reproduced, distributed, or transmitted in any form or by any means, including photocopying, recording, or other electronic or mechanical methods, without the prior written permission of the author, except in the case of brief quotations embodied in reviews, articles, or scholarly works.

This publication is a work of original authorship. All content, including but not limited to text, concepts, and structure, is the intellectual property of the author and is protected under applicable copyright laws. Unauthorized use, reproduction, or distribution of this material is strictly prohibited and may result in legal action.

Although every effort has been made to ensure the accuracy and completeness of the content, the author makes no representations or warranties of any kind and assumes no liability for any errors, omissions, or outcomes related to the use of this work.

# TABLE OF CONTENTS

**INTRODUCTION TO YELLOWSTONE** ........................................................................................... 7
    A Warm Welcome to the Park ........................................................................................... 7
    Yellowstone's Historical Legacy ........................................................................................ 8
    The Geothermal Marvels of Yellowstone ........................................................................ 8
    Wildlife Abundance and Ecological Diversity ................................................................ 9
    Unique Geological Formations and Scenic Landscapes ................................................ 9
    Rich Ecosystem Interactions ........................................................................................... 10
    Quick Facts and Seasonal Insights ................................................................................. 10
    The Cultural and Scientific Significance of Yellowstone ............................................ 11
    Immersing Yourself in the Yellowstone Experience ................................................... 11
    Appreciating the Scale and Majesty of Yellowstone ................................................... 12
    The Beauty of Seasonal Transformation ...................................................................... 12
    The Role of Yellowstone in the Modern World .......................................................... 13
    Embracing the Spirit of Exploration ............................................................................. 13
    Practicing Responsible Tourism and Stewardship ..................................................... 14
    Savoring Every Moment in Yellowstone ..................................................................... 14

**PLANNING YOUR TRIP** ............................................................................................................. 17
    When to Visit: Timing Your Adventure ....................................................................... 17
    How to Get There: Navigating to America's First National Park .............................. 18
    Park Passes & Entrance Fees: Preparing for Your Stay .............................................. 19
    Crafting Your Itinerary: Balancing Adventure and Preparation ............................... 20
    Budgeting and Practical Considerations ...................................................................... 21
    Preparing Documentation and Essential Items ........................................................... 22
    Leveraging Local Resources for a Seamless Experience ............................................ 22
    Crafting Flexibility into a Detailed Plan ....................................................................... 23
    Preparing Mentally and Physically for the Journey ................................................... 23
    Finalizing Your Pre-Trip Checklist ............................................................................... 24

**TOP ATTRACTIONS & MUST-SEE SPOTS** ............................................................................. 26
    Old Faithful: The Icon of Yellowstone ......................................................................... 26
    Grand Prismatic Spring: Nature's Kaleidoscope ......................................................... 27
    Mammoth Hot Springs: A Journey Through Time ..................................................... 28

Yellowstone Lake: A Tranquil Waterside Retreat ........................................................... 29

　　Wildlife Viewing in Lamar and Hayden Valleys ............................................................ 30

　　Insider Tips for a Memorable Encounter ...................................................................... 32

　　Integrating Nature, History, and Adventure ................................................................. 33

**SCENIC DRIVES & HIKING TRAILS** ........................................................................... **35**

　　Scenic Drives & Hiking Trails in Yellowstone National Park ......................................... 35

　　Exploring the Scenic Drives ......................................................................................... 35

　　Hiking Trails: On Foot Through Yellowstone's Wonders ............................................... 37

　　Practical Information for Scenic Drives and Hiking Trails ............................................ 40

　　Experiencing the Intersection of Scenic Drives and Hiking Trails ................................ 42

　　Concluding With Lasting Impressions ......................................................................... 45

**CAMPING & ACCOMMODATIONS** ............................................................................ **46**

　　Exploring Camping & Accommodations in Yellowstone ............................................... 46

　　Campgrounds: The Traditional Yellowstone Camping Experience ............................... 46

　　RV Camping: Navigating the Roads with Comfort and Convenience ........................... 47

　　Lodges: Experiencing the Comforts of Historic Charm ................................................ 48

　　Reservation Systems and Strategic Planning ............................................................... 48

　　Packing Essentials and Seasonal Gear: Preparing for Every Adventure ....................... 49

　　Family-Friendly Camping and Accommodation Tips .................................................... 50

　　Guidelines for Responsible and Safe Camping ............................................................ 50

　　Seasonal Considerations for Camping and Accommodations ...................................... 51

　　Insider Tips for Securing the Perfect Spot ................................................................... 52

　　Practical Considerations and Preparations .................................................................. 52

　　Balancing Comfort and Authenticity ............................................................................ 53

　　The Role of Local Expertise and Park Resources ......................................................... 53

　　Weather Preparedness and Its Impact on **Accommodations** .................................. 54

　　Enhancing the Experience Through Thoughtful Details .............................................. 54

　　Maintaining a Connection with Nature and Community .............................................. 55

　　Embracing the Journey Through Mindful Preparation ................................................ 55

　　Final Thoughts on a Responsive and Inspiring Stay .................................................... 56

**MAPS & ITINERARIES** .............................................................................................. **57**

　　Overview of Yellowstone's Mapping System ............................................................... 57

　　Interactive Tools and Digital Resources ...................................................................... 58

　　Essential Elements for a Customized Visit .................................................................. 58

　　Detailed Park Map Overview ....................................................................................... 59

How to Navigate Yellowstone Using Maps ........................................................................................................ 59

Suggested Itineraries for Every Traveler ........................................................................................................... 59

Tailored Itineraries for Specific Interests and Demographics ........................................................................... 61

Planning Multi-Day Adventures with Integrated Mapping ............................................................................... 62

Utilizing Detailed Trail Maps for Scenic Driving and **Hiking** ............................................................................ 63

Incorporating Local Insights into Itineraries .................................................................................................... 63

Creating a Versatile Itinerary for Every Interest ............................................................................................... 64

Tips for Customizing Your Itinerary .................................................................................................................. 64

Maps and Itineraries: Integrating Practical Safety and Enjoyment .................................................................. 65

Finalizing Your Yellowstone Adventure Plans ................................................................................................... 65

## SAFETY TIPS & PARK RULES ............................................................................................................................. 67

Understanding Yellowstone's Uniquely Dynamic Environment ....................................................................... 67

Wildlife Safety: Respecting the Park's Iconic Inhabitants ................................................................................ 68

Thermal Area Cautions: Appreciating Natural Wonders from a Safe Distance ................................................ 69

Weather Awareness and Emergency Preparedness ......................................................................................... 69

Road Safety and Navigating the Park's Highways ............................................................................................ 70

Emergency Contact and Communication Protocols ........................................................................................ 71

Leave No Trace Principles and Responsible Tourism ....................................................................................... 72

Guidelines for Camping and Outdoor Activities ............................................................................................... 73

Complying with General Park Regulations ....................................................................................................... 74

Safety Practices for Specialized Activities ........................................................................................................ 75

Managing Interpersonal Health and Group Dynamics .................................................................................... 76

Interaction with the Natural World Through a Lens of Safety ......................................................................... 76

## FUN & EDUCATIONAL ACTIVITIES ..................................................................................................................... 78

Junior Ranger Program: Igniting Curiosity and Stewardship ............................................................................ 78

Capturing Yellowstone: Photography and Nature Journaling .......................................................................... 79

Stargazing: A Celestial Classroom Under the Big Sky ....................................................................................... 79

Picnic Areas and Natural Learning Zones ......................................................................................................... 80

Ranger-Led Tours: Exploring Yellowstone Through Expert Eyes ...................................................................... 80

Interactive Visitor Centers and Educational Exhibits ....................................................................................... 81

Family Exploration Challenges: Scavenger Hunts and Nature Trails ................................................................ 82

Seasonal Workshops and Special Programs ..................................................................................................... 82

Engaging with the Natural World: Environmental Education Activities ........................................................... 83

Exploring Through Technology: Mobile Apps and Digital Learning ................................................................. 84

Celebrating the Natural Heritage: Art, Culture, and History Programs ............................................................ 84

Engaging with Local Experts: Field Classes and Citizen Science ........................................................... 85
Combining Learning with Leisure: Tailored Family Itineraries ............................................................... 85
Encouraging Lifelong Learning: Resources and Continuing Engagement ............................................. 86
Bringing It Together: Practical Tips for Engaging Activities ................................................................... 86
Blueprints for a Memorable Experience ..................................................................................................... 86

## NEARBY ATTRACTIONS & DAY TRIPS ........................................................................................ 89
Exploring Beyond Yellowstone: Nearby Attractions & Day Trips ......................................................... 89
Grand Teton National Park: A Natural Masterpiece ................................................................................ 89
Cody, Wyoming: Stepping Back in Time ................................................................................................... 90
Jackson Hole: The Gateway to the West .................................................................................................... 91
Scenic Routes and Additional Day Trips ................................................................................................... 92

# INTRODUCTION TO YELLOWSTONE

Welcome to Yellowstone National Park, a land where the raw power of nature meets centuries of history and awe-inspiring beauty. As the first national park in the United States and one of the world's most iconic protected areas, Yellowstone offers visitors a rare glimpse into a dynamic ecosystem defined by its geothermal wonders, diverse wildlife, and dramatic landscapes. This introduction will immerse you in the park's storied past and reveal what makes Yellowstone a destination like no other.

From the moment you set foot in Yellowstone, you step into a living tapestry of natural history. The park's sprawling expanse covers more than 2.2 million acres, bringing together rugged mountains, vast forests, shimmering lakes, and a pulsating geothermal heart that has fascinated travelers for centuries. Yellowstone is not just a park—it is a living, breathing natural museum where visitors can witness the forces that have shaped the Earth since time immemorial.

## A Warm Welcome to the Park

Taking a journey into Yellowstone is like opening a door to a realm where every detail speaks of nature's relentless creativity and vitality. The park's striking views and immersive experiences create an immediate sense of wonder and reverence. For many, stepping into Yellowstone represents a transformation: a break from everyday concerns and an opportunity to reconnect with nature's majesty. Whether you are an avid naturalist, a family seeking a peaceful retreat, or an adventurous traveler ready to explore off-the-beaten-path wonders, Yellowstone welcomes you with open arms and endless possibilities for discovery.

The initial encounter with Yellowstone is filled with contrasts. There are moments of serene tranquility—quiet mornings by a mist-covered lake or a leisurely drive along a winding road lined with old-growth forests—and bursts of exhilarating activity, such as witnessing an erupting geyser or observing a herd of bison moving gracefully across a valley. This interplay of calm and excitement defines the very essence of Yellowstone and is a precursor to the experiences that await throughout your journey.

## Yellowstone's Historical Legacy

Yellowstone's history is as rich and multifaceted as its diverse landscapes. Established in 1872 as America's first national park, Yellowstone marked a turning point in how society values and preserves natural landscapes for public enjoyment and future generations. The decision to protect this unspoiled wilderness was revolutionary and set the stage for the modern conservation movement. Government officials, explorers, and early naturalists recognized that the park's geothermal features and abundant wildlife demanded protection, and in so doing, they ignited a passion that continues to resonate with conservationists around the globe.

Before becoming a sanctuary for nature, Yellowstone was home to Native American tribes who used the land for spiritual and practical purposes. These indigenous peoples have passed down traditions and stories that are interwoven with the park's identity, adding a layer of cultural richness to its natural beauty. Their deep connection to the land—marked by rituals, respect for nature's rhythms, and an understanding of the delicate balance between man and the environment—offers modern visitors intriguing insights into the human dimensions of Yellowstone's story.

The park's establishment was not without controversy and challenge. Debates over land use, resource management, and the clash between industrial interests and preservationist ideals framed early discussions about Yellowstone. Yet the resolve to keep Yellowstone pristine prevailed, forming a legacy that honors both natural wonders and the wisdom of past generations. This historical backdrop enhances every view, every trail, and every bubbling spring, inviting visitors to experience not only the visual splendor of the park but also its profound cultural and historical significance.

## The Geothermal Marvels of Yellowstone

One of the most distinctive features of Yellowstone is its unparalleled geothermal activity, a phenomenon that is both powerful and mesmerizing. The park sits atop a super volcano, giving rise to a landscape dotted with geysers, hot springs, fumaroles, and mud pots. Among these, Old Faithful stands out as a global icon. Its regular and predictable eruptions, shooting scalding water high into the air, have become synonymous with the very idea of Yellowstone. Yet, Old Faithful is just one of many geothermal wonders that offer visitors a firsthand look at the planet's inner workings.

Every geothermal feature in Yellowstone tells a story of deep-earth processes and the ceaseless dance of heat and water underground. The Grand Prismatic Spring, with its vivid rings of blue, green, and orange, is an artistic masterpiece painted by nature itself. The changing hues are a reflection of microbial life thriving in the mineral-rich waters, creating a living canvas that shifts with the light and temperature. This interplay of science and art is a testament to Yellowstone's uniqueness and its ability to bridge disciplines—from geology to biology, and even art and photography.

Witnessing these geothermal phenomena is not only visually captivating but also educational. Guided tours and informative exhibits help visitors understand the complex science behind these features, revealing how tiny shifts in underground pressures can result in the spectacular display of nature's power. The geothermal areas of Yellowstone serve as both natural laboratories and living art installations, celebrating Earth's capacity for both beauty and ferocity in every burst and bubble.

## Wildlife Abundance and Ecological Diversity

Yellowstone is home to an astonishing variety of wildlife, making it one of the finest natural observatories in North America. The park's ecosystems provide habitats for large mammals like bison, elk, and grizzly bears, as well as more elusive species such as wolves and lynx. This rich tapestry of fauna is a direct result of Yellowstone's commitment to conservation and the careful balance maintained by its dynamic ecosystems.

The park's wildlife can be observed in numerous settings: from the rolling meadows of Lamar Valley, where herds of bison move in a timeless rhythm, to the forested areas where bears forage and fish are caught in rushing streams. Each sighting is a reminder of the intricate food webs and natural cycles that sustain the park's many inhabitants. Wildlife enthusiasts, amateur photographers, and families with children will find endless opportunities to experience nature at its most raw and unmediated.

Guided hikes and ranger-led tours offer valuable insights into the behavior and habits of Yellowstone's wildlife, ensuring that encounters remain safe and respectful. These educational experiences emphasize the importance of maintaining a safe distance and underscore the delicate balance between observation and interference. The presence of apex predators and keystone species in the park also highlights essential ecological lessons about conservation, the propagation of species, and the ever-changing dynamics of natural habitats.

## Unique Geological Formations and Scenic Landscapes

Yellowstone's geography is a dramatic symphony of valleys, mountains, rivers, and plains, each contributing to the park's distinctive character. Its geological formations are not static relics but are constantly evolving under the influence of tectonic forces and weathering processes. The formations provide visual narratives of monumental events—from ancient volcanic eruptions to thousands of years of glacial sculpting. These stories of transformation are etched into the landscape and can be read along every trail and viewed at every overlook.

The geological story of Yellowstone is evident in features such as the colorful terraces of Mammoth Hot Springs, where mineral deposits have created intricate patterns over centuries. The contrast of vibrant travertine against the backdrop of rugged rock formations serves as a vivid illustration of the interplay between fire and water. By exploring these areas, visitors are invited to imagine the dynamic processes that continue to shape the Earth, creating features that are both timeless and ever- changing.

Each region within Yellowstone offers its own set of vistas. The expansive Yellowstone Lake shimmers under the sun, reflecting both the sky above and the hidden depths below. Meanwhile, the dramatic Grand Canyon of the Yellowstone, with its steep walls and powerful waterfalls, captures the imagination with its display of natural artistry. Every panoramic view is an invitation to pause, reflect, and appreciate the scale at which natural forces have been at work here for millennia.

## Rich Ecosystem Interactions

The remarkable tapestry of life within Yellowstone is woven together by a network of interdependent relationships. The park's flora, ranging from resilient wildflowers and robust conifers to delicate alpine blooms, creates a verdant mosaic that shifts with the seasons. This botanical diversity lays the groundwork for a healthy ecosystem where each plant contributes to soil stabilization, water filtration, and the overall aesthetic appeal of the park.

Yellowstone's ecosystems are finely tuned to the rhythms of the seasons. In the spring, the park bursts into life as snowmelt fuels vibrant displays of green and the first wildflowers courageously break through the thawing ground. Summer brings long daylight hours, allowing both flora and fauna to thrive in a climate of abundance and warmth. As autumn approaches, the landscape is transformed into a riot of colors, with golden aspens and crimson maples creating a dramatic transition before the winter's silence descends over the park. This seasonal transformation is not only visually striking but also essential for the reproductive cycles and survival strategies of the park's many species.

The interrelationships within Yellowstone extend beyond simple coexistence. Predatory cycles, migratory patterns, and even symbiotic partnerships among plant and animal species form a complex web that sustains the entire ecosystem. Observing these interactions up close provides insight into the intrinsic balance that nature maintains, ensuring that every creature, from the tiniest insect to the largest mammal, plays a role in the enduring health of the environment.

## Quick Facts and Seasonal Insights

To fully appreciate the depth and breadth of Yellowstone, it is essential to understand some quick facts and seasonal insights that shape the visitor experience. Yellowstone experiences a wide range of climates due to its vast size and varied landscape.

Summers are typically warm with long days, offering optimal conditions for hiking, camping, and wildlife viewing. However, summer also brings larger crowds and more popular tourist sites can become busy. Being prepared for these conditions, such as carrying layered clothing and plenty of water, is vital for a comfortable visit.

Spring and fall are transitional seasons that highlight dramatic shifts in weather and light. Spring is a time of renewal when snow begins to melt and the park's lower elevations burst with new life. Conversely, fall is marked by cooler temperatures and a stunning display of autumn colors, making these shoulder seasons ideal for those who prefer a quieter experience while still enjoying comfortable weather. Winter in Yellowstone, with its snow-blanketed vistas and pristine silence, offers a contrast that is both challenging and deeply rewarding. Winter travelers often engage in snowshoeing or cross-country skiing, experiencing the park in a tranquil and almost otherworldly state.

Understanding seasonal variations is key to planning the ideal adventure. The park's geyser basins, for instance, are accessible year-round, yet certain thermal features can appear dramatically different when partially frozen in winter or steaming vigorously in the summer heat. Wildlife patterns also shift with the seasons; herds may migrate to higher elevations during the summer months in search of grazing areas, while winter sees animals conserving energy and seeking shelter. These seasonal dynamics ensure that Yellowstone's landscape is never static, offering a fresh perspective with every visit.

Additionally, visitors should be aware of the unpredictable weather that can occur in Yellowstone. High altitudes and varied terrain can lead to sudden changes in temperature and weather conditions, making it essential to check forecasts and be prepared for extremes. Whether planning a family outing in summer or a more adventurous expedition in the brisk fall air, understanding these seasonal insights will equip you with the knowledge needed to adapt, explore safely, and truly appreciate the multifaceted character of this legendary park.

## The Cultural and Scientific Significance of Yellowstone

Beyond its breathtaking physical attributes, Yellowstone represents a cultural and scientific touchstone that resonates with researchers, environmentalists, and visitors alike. The park is not only a repository of natural wonders but also a living laboratory where the interplay of geology, ecology, and climate phenomena are studied in depth. Researchers from around the world are drawn to Yellowstone to study its geothermal systems, examine the effects of climate change on its flora and fauna, and understand the complex interplay of its ecosystems.

In many ways, Yellowstone epitomizes the spirit of discovery. Early explorers, scientists, and even everyday travelers have been inspired by its unparalleled landscapes. It has served as the backdrop for studies of volcanic activity and has contributed significantly to our understanding of supervolcano dynamics. The ongoing research in Yellowstone has yielded insights into geothermal energy, microbial life in extreme conditions, and even the behavior of ecosystems in response to environmental stress. Throughout its history, the park has been at the forefront of conservation science and has helped shape the policies and practices that govern protected natural areas around the globe.

Culturally, Yellowstone holds a mirror to how humanity perceives nature. It embodies the timeless notion of wilderness as a source of inspiration, introspection, and rejuvenation. Art, literature, and photography have all been profoundly influenced by the park's dramatic scenery and the evocative stories associated with its landscapes.

Every geyser eruption, every dramatic canyon vista, and every quiet moment in the shadow of ancient trees contributes to a collective narrative that transcends generations. Travelers leave Yellowstone not only with memories of spectacular vistas but also with a renewed sense of wonder about the natural world and a deeper appreciation for the heritage of the land.

## Immersing Yourself in the Yellowstone Experience

Visiting Yellowstone is a transformative experience that engages all the senses. The crisp mountain air, the gentle roar of distant geysers, and the vibrant colors of lifelike landscapes create an immersive environment that draws you in from the moment you arrive. Walking along a trail that winds through ancient forests or sitting in quiet contemplation at the edge of a steaming hot spring, the park's atmosphere is one of quiet strength and unyielding natural beauty. It invites introspection, encourages exploration, and promotes a lasting connection to the environment.

As you immerse yourself in Yellowstone, it becomes clear that the park is a place of endless discovery. Each path reveals new wonders—hidden waterfalls, secluded pools, intricate rock formations—and every turn offers another opportunity to learn more about the natural processes that have sculpted the land over millennia. The park's design and management also ensure that these experiences are accessible to everyone. Whether you are a seasoned backpacker, a family with young explorers, or a visitor just looking for a leisurely drive with breathtaking views, Yellowstone has something unique to offer each person who visits its boundaries.

One of the most engaging facets of Yellowstone is the opportunity to learn from the land itself. Signage at key locations, detailed visitor centers, and interactive exhibits all contribute to a richer understanding of the environment. Storytelling, whether conveyed through the narratives of park rangers or through interpretive displays, connects visitors to the history and science behind the park's features. This educational approach, combined with the visceral experience of being in nature, creates a memorable journey filled with insights and personal revelations.

In addition to its natural attractions, Yellowstone is a place of human connection. Meeting fellow travelers, sharing stories around a campfire, and bonding over the shared wonder of watching erupting geysers or witnessing a serene sunrise over a pristine lake—these moments strengthen the community of nature lovers who find solace and inspiration in this vast wilderness. The park's capacity to bring people together, while offering ample solitude in its expansive landscapes, is a key element of its enduring appeal.

## Appreciating the Scale and Majesty of Yellowstone

There is an unmistakable grandeur to Yellowstone that is both humbling and invigorating. Its massive expanse, dotted with iconic landmarks and hidden treasures, challenges visitors to contemplate the scale of nature's grandeur. Standing beside the roaring falls in the Grand Canyon of the Yellowstone or witnessing the vast herds roaming the open plains, one cannot help but feel a profound sense of insignificance in the face of such sublime beauty. Yet, that very feeling of being part of something much larger than oneself is what makes Yellowstone so transformative.

The park's scale is reflected in the diversity of experiences available. On one day, you might traverse winding roads that reveal panoramic vistas of rugged mountains and sweeping valleys. On another, you might delve into the geothermal corridors where hot springs bubble and steam rises in delicate swirls against a bright blue sky. Each microcosm within the park is a world unto itself, demanding both quiet contemplation and active exploration. This blend of macro and micro perspectives enriches the overall experience, providing a tapestry of images and sensations that are both deeply personal and universally awe-inspiring.

Traveling through Yellowstone is also an exercise in discovery. As you move from one area of the park to another, you begin to understand the interconnectedness of its features. The roaring, geothermal energy of one basin eventually gives way to the still beauty of a high mountain lake. The persistent cycles of wildlife behavior echo the persistent forces of geological change. In this interplay of contrasting elements, Yellowstone offers a living demonstration of nature's resilience and beauty—a place where each visitor is invited to explore, learn, and grow.

## The Beauty of Seasonal Transformation

One of the most enchanting aspects of Yellowstone is its ability to transform with the passing of the seasons. Each season paints the park in a different light and mood, offering a range of experiences that highlight its versatility and enduring allure.

Summer, with its long golden days and warm embrace, provides visitors with ample time for outdoor adventures, from hiking and kayaking to wildlife watching during the early morning hours. The long days allow for prolonged exploration, making it possible to witness multiple natural marvels in a single visit.

As the park transitions into autumn, the landscape is set ablaze with color. The deciduous trees, having spent the summer absorbing the sun's bounty, begin to turn vivid hues of red, orange, and gold. This seasonal metamorphosis not only creates a visual feast for photographers and nature enthusiasts alike but also signals the beginning of quieter times in the park. The cooler temperatures and reduced crowds in the fall afford a more reflective and intimate encounter with nature, as the days shorten and the chill of approaching winter begins to stir.

When winter arrives, Yellowstone enters a realm of pristine solitude. Snow blankets the ground, softening the contours of rocky outcrops and diminishing the distance between the visitor and the wilderness. The geothermal areas, resilient as ever, continue to bubble and steam against the background of a white, crystalline landscape. The contrast of iron-steel blues and whites is nothing short of magical, creating an atmosphere that is both serene and invigorating. For those willing to brave the cold, winter in Yellowstone offers a unique and deeply personal experience—a chance to witness nature's quiet strength in its most undisturbed form.

Early spring brings with it the promise of renewal. The melting snow feeds mighty rivers and streams, awakening the park's flora and fauna after a long dormancy. The rhythmic sound of flowing water, intermingled with the gradual emergence of green shoots and blossoms, marks the beginning of a new cycle of life. Each season has its own charm and challenges, and understanding these seasonal shifts is key to planning an experience at Yellowstone that is both safe and satisfying.

## The Role of Yellowstone in the Modern World

In today's rapidly changing world, Yellowstone stands as a testament to the enduring importance of conservation. Its existence as a protected land has influenced environmental policies and nurtured a broader public appreciation for nature. The park represents a commitment to preserving natural heritage amidst the pressures of urbanization and industrial growth. It is a living reminder that safeguarding wild spaces is not only a matter of environmental stewardship but also a celebration of the beauty and complexity of life.

Modern visitors to Yellowstone are invited to participate in a legacy of conservation and exploration that spans generations. Park management works tirelessly to balance the needs of tourists with the necessity of protecting delicate ecological networks.

Strategies such as visitor education, habitat restoration, and wildlife monitoring are integral to ensuring that Yellowstone remains a vibrant ecosystem for future generations. This dedication to preservation is palpable throughout the park, from the informational displays at visitor centers to the heartfelt guidance provided by park rangers during tours.

The lessons learned from Yellowstone resonate far beyond its borders. The park's history of conservation has influenced national policies and international discussions on environmental protection. Yellowstone is not only a destination for voyage and exploration but also a living classroom where the principles of sustainability, scientific inquiry, and responsible tourism are put into practice. Visitors leave the park with a deeper understanding of the intrinsic value of nature and the shared responsibility of maintaining and nurturing the planet's fragile ecosystems.

## Embracing the Spirit of Exploration

Yellowstone thrives on the spirit of exploration, an ethos that invites every visitor to become a part of its continuing story. Each trail, geyser, and valley offers an invitation to engage directly with nature. This sense of adventure is deeply embedded in the park's ethos—from the early explorers who first mapped its terrain to today's hikers, campers, and family travelers who actively seek out the hidden corners of this spectacular landscape.

Embracing the spirit of exploration means approaching Yellowstone with both a sense of wonder and a measure of preparedness. It encourages visitors to venture beyond the well-trodden paths and experience the park's more secluded areas. Whether it is through a quiet morning paddle on a remote lake or a leisurely walk through lesser-known geothermal zones, every journey adds a new dimension to your understanding and appreciation of Yellowstone. The park's vastness offers the perfect backdrop for personal discovery, where moments of solitude and periods of dynamic activity work together to create a memorable adventure.

For those seeking an active exploration, Yellowstone's extensive network of trails caters to a wide range of abilities and interests. From short, easily accessible loops perfect for families with children to longer, more challenging routes ideal for experienced hikers, the park encourages you to set your own pace and discover the natural wonders that lie just off the beaten path. Interpretation centers, ranger-led activities, and well-designed signage help ensure that you can enjoy these adventures safely while gaining deeper insights into the environmental significance of each location.

## Practicing Responsible Tourism and Stewardship

One of the enduring values of Yellowstone is the emphasis on responsible tourism and stewardship. As a sanctuary of both natural beauty and scientific discovery, the park operates under principles that prioritize conservation, safety, and respect for the environment. Visitors are encouraged to abide by park guidelines that ensure the delicate balance between human recreation and the need to maintain pristine natural conditions.

Being a responsible visitor in Yellowstone involves simple yet powerful actions: keeping a safe distance from wildlife, following designated trails, and practicing Leave No Trace principles. These practices help protect fragile habitats and ensure that Yellowstone continues to be a living wonder for both current and future generations. Park rangers and educators are always available to provide guidance on how best to interact with the environment, turning a day of exploration into an educational experience that reinforces the value of conservation ethics.

Programs aimed at wildlife preservation, habitat restoration, and educational outreach allow visitors to engage directly with the park's ongoing efforts to sustain its natural beauty. Whether volunteering for a local conservation project or simply digesting the wealth of interpretive information available at visitor centers, every action contributes to a broader collective effort to preserve Yellowstone. The park's commitment to sustainable tourism serves as a model for protected areas worldwide, emphasizing that the enjoyment of nature is inseparable from the responsibility to care for its future.

## Savoring Every Moment in Yellowstone

Yellowstone's allure lies not only in its grand vistas and dramatic geological features but also in the subtle, quiet moments that punctuate every visit. The park invites you to slow down and savor those moments that are easily overlooked in the rush of daily life—a glimmering reflection on a still pond, the gentle rustling of leaves in a secluded grove, or the soft murmur of distant wildlife at dusk. These intimate encounters with nature form a personal narrative of connection and inspiration, enabling you to leave a part of your heart in the wilderness.

The park's design as both a recreational haven and a living museum of natural history means that every experience is layered with opportunities for appreciation. Listen to the stories carried on the wind, see the traces of ancient fires and glacial movements in the rock formations, and feel the warmth of the thermal springs on your skin. These sensory experiences combine to create a holistic picture of Yellowstone that transcends simple description—an evolving narrative told by the land itself.

Local experts and longtime residents often speak of the park as a place where time both stands still and moves in rhythmic cycles. Embracing this fluidity means understanding that every visit to Yellowstone is unique. No two days are exactly alike, and the park's ever-changing character encourages you to adopt an open perspective, ready to absorb the myriad details that define each moment. Whether you encounter a sudden burst of geothermal energy, a fleeting glimpse of a wild animal in its natural habitat, or a solitary sunrise over a vast plain, each experience is an invitation to celebrate the wonder of the natural world.

A thoughtful approach to exploring Yellowstone involves both preparation and presence. By reading up on the park's history, understanding its natural processes, and equipping yourself with maps and tips, you lay the groundwork for an effective and enriching adventure. Equally important is the mindful appreciation of every sensory detail—observing, questioning, and feeling the pulse of a landscape that has inspired generations of explorers and naturalists. The park is a repository of stories, both ancient and new, each waiting to be discovered by those who are willing to look closely and listen intently.

Yellowstone is a celebration of nature's resilience and adaptation. It is a destination that not only offers a feast for the eyes but also a playground for the mind and soul. Every path you tread, every geyser you observe, and every animal encounter you experience adds new chapters to your personal journey. With every step, the park opens its doors to discoveries that are as much about the natural world as they are about your own journey of exploration.

In this incredible landscape, learning never ceases, and inspiration is always within reach. The blend of geological marvels, thriving wildlife, and the persistent spirit of conservation creates an environment that is both local and universal—a place where every visitor is reminded of the power, beauty, and complexity of the Earth. The interplay of elements, the cycles of seasons, and the sheer scale of the wilderness encourage a reevaluation of one's place in the natural order, fostering a deep sense of respect for the delicate balance shared by all living things.

Each sunrise over Yellowstone is a promise of potential, echoing the countless stories of exploration and discovery that have unfolded over the centuries. As you traverse the diverse landscapes—from rugged mountain trails and verdant valleys to steaming thermal springs and crystal-clear lakes—you are not merely a visitor, but a crucial participant in a dynamic narrative of nature that continues to evolve. The park fosters a steady dialogue between past and present, tradition and innovation, urging you to delve into both the scientific mysteries and the timeless beauty that make Yellowstone an enduring symbol of wild America. Being in Yellowstone is a privilege that comes with both exhilaration and responsibility. Its legacy's weight reminds us that such natural wonders require careful stewardship and mindful engagement. The lessons learned here extend beyond the park's borders, influencing personal perspectives on environmental care, community involvement, and the intrinsic value of untouched nature. Embrace the opportunity to reflect on these larger themes as you wander the trails, observe the geysers, and breathe in the crisp, invigorating air of Yellowstone.

This vast and ancient landscape has weathered countless changes, yet it remains a sanctuary of resilience and renewal. Every rock formation tells tales of primordial events, every bubbling spring echoes the Earth's interior, and every living creature contributes to the park's vibrant ecosystem. Yellowstone symbolizes not only a tribute to natural beauty but also humanity's enduring commitment to recognizing and preserving the majesty of our planet. As you continue to explore its boundless beauty, you become part of a living tradition—a legacy of engagement with nature that enriches both the individual and the collective understanding of wilderness.

In your journey through Yellowstone, each step invites reflection on the intricate interplay between natural forces and human curiosity. From the thunderous eruptions of geysers to the quiet rustle of wildlife in the meadows, the park offers moments of introspection and exhilaration alike. The layered history, vibrant ecosystems, and unparalleled natural phenomena coalesce to form a virtually endless canvas for exploration and inspiration. With every new vista uncovered and every subtle detail noticed, Yellowstone asserts its dominion as one of the world's most remarkable natural reserves—a beacon of natural wonder that continues to challenge, inspire, and endure.

Every visit to Yellowstone is a rediscovery of life's intrinsic beauty—a call to reconnect with a world that is both ancient and timeless. As you prepare to embark deeper into the wonders that lie ahead, let the grandeur of Yellowstone remind you of the profound lessons embedded in its landscapes. The park stands as a testimony to the majesty of nature, a reminder that even in the most dynamic and ever-changing environments, there is a continuity of beauty and mystery that enriches all who take the time to explore it.

# PLANNING YOUR TRIP

Planning your adventure to Yellowstone National Park is much more than simply picking a date and packing your bags. It is an intricate process that involves meticulous research, flexibility with the weather and park events, and a thorough understanding of the park's seasonal characteristics. As you prepare for your journey, consider every detail—from the best time of year to visit and reliable routes to access the park, to the administrative steps needed such as obtaining park passes and understanding entrance fees. This section provides a detailed roadmap to ensure that your Yellowstone experience begins with a smooth and well-informed planning process.

## When to Visit: Timing Your Adventure

Yellowstone's diverse landscape and ever-changing climate mean that every season produces its own character and unique set of experiences. A comprehensive understanding of each season's benefits and challenges is crucial for tailoring your visit to your personal interests and physical capabilities.

**Spring** in Yellowstone is a time of renewal. As the park emerges from its winter slumber, the melting snow revives the bubbling streams and rivers. Wildlife becomes more visible as animals emerge from hibernation or begin their annual migrations.

However, spring can also be unpredictable. Snow and rain may persist in some areas, and some roads may only be partially open. For travelers who prefer fewer crowds and want to witness newborn animals and blossoming wildflowers, spring offers a magical introductory stage to Yellowstone's vibrant ecosystems. When planning a spring visit, ensure that your itinerary contains flexible activities; some trails might be closed due to lingering snow, while some geyser basins could have variable water levels influenced by the melting process.

**Summer** is undoubtedly the peak season for Yellowstone visitors. With nearly every park facility fully operational, families and outdoor enthusiasts flock to the park to enjoy the long, sunlit days and a plethora of park activities. The weather is generally the most favorable, with warm days and cool nights that create a perfect climate for hiking, camping, and wildlife viewing. One of the primary benefits of a summer trip is the nearly complete access to all roads, trails, and attractions, including the frequently visited geyser basins and stunning scenic drives. However, the popularity of the park during these months also means increased visitor numbers, which can lead to crowded viewpoints and longer waits at iconic sites like Old Faithful. For those visiting in summer, it is wise to develop a detailed daily itinerary that accounts for early arrivals and off-peak hours to experience the park's natural wonders at their serene best.

**Fall** offers a quieter, more introspective experience in Yellowstone. The changing leaves lend the park a surreal palette of reds, oranges, and golds, and the crisp air enhances every outdoor activity. Fall is an ideal time for photographers and nature lovers eager to capture Yellowstone's transformative beauty. The seasonal migration of animals, particularly bison and elk, provides excellent opportunities for wildlife observation. Additionally, the fewer crowds allow for a more relaxed exploration of popular attractions. Keep in mind, though, that some park services may start scaling back operations as temperatures drop and snow begins to form on higher elevations. Road closures, especially in mountainous regions, can start early depending on the year's specific weather patterns. When planning a visit during the fall, verify the status of roads and facilities ahead of time, and consider contacting the park's visitor center regularly for updated information.

**Winter** in Yellowstone is an entirely different adventure. The park is transformed into a pristine, snow-covered wonderland, where tranquility and stark beauty reign supreme. Winter visits are perfect for those who appreciate solitude and are eager to explore the park's landscapes under dramatically quiet conditions. However, the harsh weather and limited accessibility to many areas of the park create challenges.

Most roads are closed to regular vehicles, and visitors must rely on guided snowmobile and snowcoach tours to see the park's famous geysers and unique thermal features. Winter conditions also mean a higher level of preparedness is essential—think about carrying emergency gear, ensuring your vehicle is equipped for treacherous conditions, and dressing in multiple layers. This season is best suited for those who are experienced in winter travel or are joining a guided tour that can navigate Yellowstone's icy roads safely.

No matter which season you prefer, planning your visit to Yellowstone requires a thorough understanding of the weather trends, anticipated visitor volumes, and park regulations for that time of year. It's essential to research historical weather data, check for any park alerts, and plan for contingencies if nature decides to change its course unexpectedly. Consider subscribing to the park's newsletter or following its official social media channels for real-time updates during your stay. Balancing your desires with practical constraints ensures that your visit, regardless of the season, is both unforgettable and safe.

## How to Get There: Navigating to America's First National Park

Yellowstone National Park spans across three states—Wyoming, Montana, and Idaho—each offering different access points and travel routes. Understanding the best methods to get to the park can add considerable ease to your planning process. Whether you are flying in from a distant location, driving from a neighboring state, or embarking on a multifaceted road trip, the journey to Yellowstone is filled with scenic routes and unique travel experiences.

**By Air:** For many travelers, air travel is the simplest way to reach the broader vicinity of Yellowstone. The nearest major airports are located in Bozeman, Montana; Jackson, Wyoming; and Idaho Falls, Idaho. Each airport offers unique benefits. For instance, Bozeman Yellowstone International Airport is the busiest and has numerous daily connections, making it a practical option for national or international travelers.

Jackson Hole Airport is smaller and ideally located for those planning to visit not only Yellowstone but also Grand Teton National Park. Additionally, the flights into Idaho Falls often provide a less congested arrival experience with ample car rental options.

Once you land, renting a car is highly recommended. A reliable vehicle provides the freedom to explore the park's vast expanses, traverse scenic backroads, and adjust your schedule to catch sunrise views at iconic landmarks. It is advisable to book your rental vehicle well in advance, particularly during peak seasons, to ensure availability and more favorable rates.

**By Car:** Embarking on a road trip to Yellowstone is an experience in itself. The drive to the park often takes you through breathtaking landscapes, charming towns, and multiple state attractions. Major highways connect most regions of the country to Yellowstone, ensuring convenience along with the liberty of a self-tailored journey.

Many travelers enjoy the added adventure that comes with a road trip, stopping at various scenic overlooks, local diners, and historical sites along the way. When planning your route, incorporate regular stops for rest and refreshments. Map out your path using the latest GPS technology combined with traditional park maps—this dual approach ensures that you remain updated on the trail conditions and any detours that might arise due to weather or maintenance work. Additionally, consider the type of vehicle best suited for the terrain. In winter, for example, vehicles with four-wheel drive and comprehensive safety features are paramount, whereas in summer, a standard SUV or a comfortable sedan may suffice.

**On the Road:** Yellowstone's road network is extensive, yet it demands a degree of caution as conditions can vary significantly within a short distance. Key routes such as the Grand Loop Road offer access to most major attractions, but certain narrower, unpaved roads lead to hidden gems deep within the park. Before you set out, check current road conditions using the National Park Service's online resources or their mobile app, which provides updated information about closures, construction, and wildlife-related delays. Even during the busy summer months, early morning drives or late evening trips can provide a quieter, more serene driving experience—and a better chance to see wildlife crossing the roads.

**Navigational Tools:** Modern technology offers a plethora of navigational aids that make traveling to Yellowstone more manageable than ever. GPS devices, park-specific mobile apps, and traditional paper maps are all invaluable tools in your journey. It is prudent to carry a physical map or guidebook along with digital devices, as some regions of the park have limited cell service. Contemporary traveler apps often include offline maps, points of interest, and real-time weather updates which can be crucial when venturing outside of populated areas. Integrating technology with traditional navigational methods prepares you for unexpected changes and ensures a safe and informed journey.

## Park Passes & Entrance Fees: Preparing for Your Stay

One of the first administrative steps in your planning process is to understand Yellowstone's fee and pass system. Yellowstone National Park is one of the most visited national parks in the United States, and its fee structure plays a significant role in maintaining its natural beauty. Preparing in advance for park passes and fees guarantees a smoother entrance experience and allows you to focus on your adventure once inside.

**Types of Passes:** Yellowstone National Park offers several types of entrance passes designed to cater to different visitation patterns and interests. The most common is the private vehicle pass, which covers entry for all passengers and is valid for seven consecutive days. For those who prefer a more flexible approach—especially if planning multiple trips throughout the year—the annual pass is a cost-effective option. There are also special passes available for military personnel and annual passes that cover use in several other national parks, such as the America the Beautiful Pass. Understanding these options is essential, as each pass offers different benefits depending on your travel style and anticipated duration of visits.

**Where to Purchase:** Passes can be purchased in a variety of ways, both online and on arrival. The official National Park Service website offers a straightforward platform for pre-purchasing your pass, which not only saves time but also allows you to avoid potential delays at the park gates during busy periods. Some regional vendors and park stores also sell passes, but for authenticity and accuracy, it is best to rely on official sources. Pre-purchasing has added advantages: in digital form, your pass can be stored on your mobile device in case you misplace the physical copy, and it integrates seamlessly with other online services to update you on park conditions and events.

**Entrance Fees:** The fee structure is designed to support conservation efforts and maintain the park's facilities. The entrance fee for a private vehicle, for example, is subject to periodic adjustments, so it is worthwhile to check the latest rates before your trip. Payment is typically accepted in multiple forms, including major credit cards and cash, though contactless payment options have gained popularity for their speed and convenience. Understanding the fee structure in detail allows you to plan your overall travel budget more accurately, ensuring that you are prepared for every expense that may arise during your Yellowstone journey.

**Conservation Contributions:** It is important to remember that these fees directly contribute to preserving Yellowstone's pristine environment. The funds are allocated toward trail maintenance, visitor services, infrastructure improvements, and wildlife management programs that ensure the long-term protection of this natural wonder. By purchasing the appropriate passes, you are not only facilitating your own entry into the park—you are also actively supporting the conservation efforts necessary to keep Yellowstone vibrant and accessible for future generations.

**Special Permits and Additional Fees:** For travelers planning to engage in special activities within the park—such as guided tours, certain camping sites, or backcountry hikes—there may be additional permits or fees required. Some sections of Yellowstone have restrictions to protect delicate ecosystems or to ensure visitor safety. It is imperative to review the park's official guidelines regarding such activities well in advance. This preparation might involve applying for a backcountry permit if your itinerary includes extended hiking or camping trips beyond designated campgrounds, or registering for a guided tour that covers hard-to-access areas. Being proactive in this regard helps avoid last-minute complications once you arrive at the park.

**Online Resources and Visitor Centers:** Yellowstone is committed to making the process of obtaining passes and permits as seamless as possible. The park's website not only provides updated information on fees but also features detailed FAQs and step-by-step guides on purchasing. Upon your arrival, visitor centers located throughout the park offer additional assistance and can help clarify any uncertainties regarding pass types, validity periods, and seasonal restrictions. These centers are an excellent resource for getting the most current updates, especially if the weather or unexpected events have affected park operations. They also offer maps, brochures, and advice on navigating the expansive park effectively.

# Crafting Your Itinerary: Balancing Adventure and Preparation

A well-crafted itinerary is the backbone of your trip planning process. Yellowstone's vast expanse and diverse attractions call for a structured plan that outlines daily activities, recommended routes, and contingency plans in case of unforeseen changes. Begin by identifying your must-see sights—be it the iconic geysers, the serene lakes, or the abundant wildlife viewing opportunities—and then build your schedule around them.

Detailing your itinerary involves evaluating travel times between attractions, factoring in rest stops, and planning for meals. Many of Yellowstone's popular attractions are dispersed over large distances, so allow ample time in your itinerary to account for the inevitable delays or detours along the scenic yet challenging park roads. Consider dividing your itinerary into themed days; for example, one day might revolve solely around geothermal features, while another is dedicated to exploring dense forests and wildlife-rich valleys. Flexibility should be built into your schedule—to change destinations if weather conditions become adverse or if a particular area turns out to be exceptionally crowded.

For families, a carefully balanced itinerary includes both educational and recreational activities. Young travelers often benefit from shorter, more interactive excursions that incorporate elements of the park's geological history or wildlife conservation efforts. Many visitor centers offer junior ranger programs or interactive exhibits, providing both learning and fun in one setting. Adults, on the other hand, might prefer longer hikes or photography sessions at quieter hours. By considering the diverse interests and energy levels within your travel group, you can tailor your itinerary to maintain engagement and minimize fatigue.

It is also helpful to incorporate breaks and downtime into your itinerary. Yellowstone's beauty is best appreciated when you take the time to sit quietly and absorb the natural surroundings. Plan for moments of relaxation—whether it's an extended picnic in a designated area, an unhurried drive along the park's backroads, or simply a pause at a scenic overlook to marvel at the expansive vistas. Such breaks not only serve as rest periods but also allow you to make spontaneous decisions to explore hidden gems that might have been missed in a rigid schedule.

## Budgeting and Practical Considerations

Proper planning extends beyond scheduling and route mapping into an area of pragmatic financial management. Yellowstone can be explored on a variety of budgets, and the cost elements involved can vary widely depending on the season, the chosen mode of transportation, and the type of accommodations you select. It is essential to evaluate the overall expenses—from travel and lodging to park fees and incidentals—so that your adventure remains both enjoyable and stress-free.

Start by estimating the cost of transportation, which includes flights or fuel for long drives, car rental fees, and any potential parking charges within the park. If booking flights, compare multiple carriers and consider travel dates that might coincide with lower fares. When renting a vehicle, additional costs such as insurance coverage and upgrades for off-road capabilities in winter should be factored into your budget. Budgeting for these expenses early in your planning phase provides a clear financial outline, which in turn helps you make adjustments to preferred activities or accommodations if necessary.

Accommodations in and around Yellowstone range from rustic campgrounds and lodges within the park to hotels in nearby gateway towns. Camping is often the most affordable option, but it requires advanced reservations, particularly in the peak summer months. For those who prefer extra comfort, lodges and hotels offer modern amenities and proximity to major park attractions. When evaluating your options, research and compare reviews, cancellation policies, and additional costs such as resort fees. Many accommodations offer package deals that include park passes or guided tours, which can further streamline your financial planning.

Meals and daily expenses should also be considered. Eating within the park can range from inexpensive picnic options to dining at lodges that offer elaborate menus. If you plan to prepare your meals, particularly if camping, include the cost of groceries and consider packing essential kitchen gear. Local markets in nearby towns often provide a mix of fresh produce, local specialties, and essentials that can add a unique culinary dimension to your trip. Balancing the splurge on one meal with budget-friendly options for others allows you to savor the unique flavors of the region without overspending.

Preparing for unexpected expenses is another vital element of practical travel planning. Whether it's a minor car repair, an emergency medical need, or simply an impromptu guided tour, having a contingency fund can alleviate stress and provide flexibility. Travel insurance is also highly recommended, as it can cover unforeseen delays, cancellations, and other emergencies that might disrupt your plans. Comparing policies from various providers and understanding what is and isn't covered gives you a comprehensive safety net for your adventure.

## Preparing Documentation and Essential Items

No comprehensive trip planning process is complete without ensuring that you have all necessary documentation and essential items. Yellowstone's remote locations demand that visitors are prepared for long days outdoors and variable weather conditions. Organizing your paperwork, maps, and travel guides ahead of time will save you time once you are on the move.

Before departing, double-check that you have all required identification, booking confirmations, and permits, particularly if engaging in backcountry adventures or specialized tours. It is advisable to have both physical copies and digital backups stored securely. This redundancy ensures that should one method fail, you are not left without the critical documents needed for a smooth visit.

Alongside your documentation, preparing a comprehensive packing list tailored to Yellowstone's conditions is crucial. Layered clothing is a must—think moisture-wicking fabrics, insulated outerwear, and sturdy hiking boots—so that you can adjust to temperature changes throughout the day. Depending on the season, additional gear such as snowshoes, trekking poles, or sun protection may be necessary. Packing a well-stocked first aid kit, portable chargers, and extra water and snacks further ensures that you are ready for any minor mishap or sudden change in your itinerary.

Since cell service can be limited in remote parts of the park, carrying a physical map of Yellowstone is an invaluable backup. Even for those who rely on GPS navigation, a detailed park map can help pinpoint attractions and hiking trails with stunning clarity. Many park maps are available at visitor centers, and some guidebooks provide specialty maps with annotated historical sites, wildlife hotspots, and lesser-known trails.

Hygiene and sustainability are also key considerations when traveling to a natural sanctuary. Bring biodegradable soaps, reusable water bottles, and other eco-friendly products to minimize the environmental footprint of your visit. Yellowstone, like many national parks, encourages visitors to embrace Leave No Trace principles— disposing of waste responsibly and minimizing impact on natural habitats. Moving forward with these preparations not only ensures practical readiness but also demonstrates respect for the preserved beauty of the park.

## Leveraging Local Resources for a Seamless Experience

Taking advantage of local resources is an essential component of successful trip planning. Yellowstone's surrounding communities boast a wealth of information that can enrich your visit. Small-town visitor centers, local tour operators, and dedicated park guides offer insights that sometimes go beyond what is available through national park literature.

Local visitor centers provide regional maps, recommendations, and updates on weather, road conditions, and seasonal events. Conversations with residents and park rangers can unearth hidden gems and off-the-beaten-path attractions that may not feature prominently in mainstream travel guides. Additionally, many of these local resources share insider tips—such as the best time to view wildlife or the optimal starting points for quiet hikes—that save precious time and enhance your overall experience.

For those with a penchant for planning ahead, online travel forums and dedicated Yellowstone websites serve as modern treasure troves of first-hand accounts and practical advice. Reading stories and reviews from travelers who have navigated the park under similar conditions provides reassurance and inspiration. Social media groups, in particular, can offer real-time updates and cautionary notes regarding weather patterns, road closures, or any unforeseen changes in park operations. Integrating these contemporary resources with traditional research not only refines your itinerary but also cultivates a sense of community among fellow adventurers.

For families and group travelers, pre-arranging guided tours and ranger-led activities is an excellent strategy. Many guided tours offer early booking discounts and package deals that combine transportation, meals, and park admission fees. By aligning group interests in advance—whether through a full-day wildlife tour or a specialized photography trip—you can secure your spot in high-demand activities, ensuring that everyone in your traveling party gains the most from Yellowstone's offerings. These localized services, steeped in the history and ecological intricacies of the park, provide a layer of depth that enhances your visit beyond the ordinary.

## Crafting Flexibility into a Detailed Plan

Even the most carefully crafted itinerary should be designed with flexibility in mind. Yellowstone is known for its dynamic natural elements—sudden changes in weather, unexpected road closures, or the spontaneous appearance of wildlife can alter your schedule in an instant. Building in buffer times within your daily itinerary allows you to accommodate these changes without feeling rushed or missing out on unexpected moments of wonder.

Consider arranging your itinerary so that no single day is overwhelming. Start with a core plan that outlines the essential destinations and must-see attractions, then leave extra hours interspersed between planned activities. Use these windows of time to explore recommended detours, take a leisurely drive along a scenic byway, or simply relax by a bubbling hot spring. This approach not only reduces the stress of sticking to a rigid schedule but also increases your opportunities to enjoy Yellowstone without the pressure of constant movement.

Flexibility also means being prepared to adapt your plans if your energy levels fluctuate or if unexpected opportunities arise. It is beneficial to have a list of backup activities—perhaps a short walk near an interpretive trail or an impromptu visit to a nearby pond—so that if your main plan is disrupted, you still have engaging alternatives. Checking in regularly with park staff and local guides throughout your day can also present new ideas or updates that may refine your original itinerary.

Embracing a flexible planning mindset is perhaps the greatest asset you can have when immersing yourself in the ever-evolving natural landscape of Yellowstone.

## Preparing Mentally and Physically for the Journey

Performance in the wilderness is not solely dependent upon physical preparedness but also on the mental state with which you approach the adventure. Yellowstone's rugged terrain and unpredictable climate present challenges that can test your endurance and resourcefulness. Preparing yourself both mentally and physically for these conditions may involve specific training regimes, rest, and even research into advanced outdoor survival skills, if applicable to your itinerary.

Prior to your trip, engaging in moderate physical activities such as hiking, cycling, or even brisk walking can build the stamina needed for long days of exploration. The park's trails vary greatly in difficulty, and having a baseline level of fitness will ensure that you appreciate every step of your journey—from climbs up steep trails to extended periods of walking through vast valleys. Additionally, studying elevation changes and terrain maps can help you set realistic daily goals. This level of physical preparation not only reduces the risk of injury but also enhances the overall enjoyment of the park's physical challenges.

Mentally, setting an attitude of curiosity and respect for nature will enrich your experience. Spend time familiarizing yourself with Yellowstone's unique ecological and geological features before you arrive. Reading articles, watching documentaries, and participating in online discussions about the park's history and natural phenomena can heighten your anticipation and prime your mind for the immersive experience that awaits. A well-prepared mind, combined with physical readiness, creates a harmonious balance that allows you to fully appreciate the subtle details of the landscapes and the profound silence of untouched wilderness.

## Finalizing Your Pre-Trip Checklist

With every element of planning addressed—from understanding seasonal variations to securing necessary permits and tailoring your itinerary to the group's interests—it is now time to consolidate all details into a cohesive pre-trip checklist. This final step bridges meticulous planning with actual execution, ensuring that no essential component is overlooked as you embark on your journey into Yellowstone.

Your pre-trip checklist should include:

- Confirmation of travel arrangements, including flight or vehicle rental details
- Copies of all necessary documentation such as park passes, permits, driver's licenses, and travel insurance policies
- A detailed itinerary for each day, including main attractions, secondary stops, and flexible time slots for spontaneous exploration
- Essential contact information, including numbers for local resources, the park's visitor centers, emergency services, and local tour operators
- A comprehensive packing list that encompasses weather-appropriate clothing, hiking gear, navigation aids (both digital and paper maps), emergency kits, and sustainability-focused travel items
- Pre-loaded digital resources such as offline maps, downloaded PDFs of park brochures, and links to relevant Yellowstone websites that offer real-time updates
- Pre-planned backup options for meals, lodging, and activities in case of unexpected weather changes or closures

By reviewing and cross-checking each item on your checklist in the weeks leading up to your departure, you create an organized framework that sets the tone for a stress- free adventure. This level of detail not only minimizes last-minute disruptions but also bolsters your confidence as you step into the great outdoors.

## Harnessing the Spirit of Adventure Through Preparedness

With every piece in place, planning your trip to Yellowstone becomes an embodiment of preparedness meeting the spirit of adventure. Navigating through the intricacies of seasonal shifts, travel logistics, and park administration mirrors the multifaceted charm of Yellowstone itself—a land where nature's grandeur and human curiosity converge. Approaching your visit with comprehensive preparation transforms potential challenges into opportunities for deeper exploration and engagement with one of America's most storied landscapes.

Leveraging these detailed insights throughout your planning process, you draw closer to understanding not only the logistics but also the essence of what makes Yellowstone so compelling. Whether you are eager for high-adrenaline hikes, contemplative moments by steaming geysers, or quiet observations of wildlife in their natural habitat, thoughtful preparation is the cornerstone of an experience that transcends ordinary travel.

By embracing proactive planning—from selecting the optimal visiting season and choosing a travel method that suits your style, to securing passes and developing an adaptable itinerary—you empower yourself to maximize every moment spent in Yellowstone's embrace. The well-prepared traveler appreciates that true adventure lies in the interplay between meticulous planning and the readiness to embrace the unexpected wonders the park has to offer. Enjoy the journey not simply as a series of movements from one attraction to another, but as an immersive dialogue with nature, enriched by local wisdom, cutting-edge navigation tools, and timeless wilderness traditions.

Taking into account all of these elements enhances not only your overall experience here at Yellowstone but also personal memories that will last a lifetime. Equipped with detailed maps, backup plans, and the adventurous spirit of discovery, you are well on your way to exploring every vibrant corner of this dynamic landscape. This phase of your preparations is a testament to the critical role that thoughtful planning plays in unleashing the full potential of your national park adventure. Enjoy the art of planning: let it infuse your journey with anticipation, flexibility, and an unwavering respect for one of nature's most celebrated treasures.

With every detail meticulously reviewed, your path to Yellowstone now unfolds as both a tangible itinerary and a mental state of readiness. The journey to America's first national park is not just about arriving—it's about embracing the adventure from the moment you board your flight, begin your drive, or pack your backpack. As you step into the welcoming expanse of Yellowstone, your detailed planning becomes an intrinsic part of the experience, ensuring that every geyser's eruption, every wildlife encounter, and every quiet moment on a scenic trail is all the richer because you took the time to prepare.

Integrated planning, realistic budgeting, continuous updates through local resources, and an adaptable itinerary are the cornerstones upon which your adventure is built. Each aspect of your trip has been finely tuned to accentuate the majesty and mystery of Yellowstone while keeping you safe, informed, and engaged. Your journey into this remarkable landscape begins with solid preparation, setting the stage for a vibrant experience that is as dynamic and awe-inspiring as the park itself.

# TOP ATTRACTIONS & MUST-SEE SPOTS

Yellowstone National Park is a living tapestry of awe-inspiring natural phenomena, a realm where the earth breathes and landscapes evolve before your very eyes. This majestic park boasts a rich array of iconic landmarks and hidden gems that coalesce to create a dynamic experience for every visitor. From the reliable spectacle of the erupting Old Faithful geyser to the ethereal colors of the Grand Prismatic Spring, and from the surreal terraces of Mammoth Hot Springs to the tranquil shores of Yellowstone Lake, each landmark tells its own vivid story. Equally captivating are the expansive wilderness areas of Lamar Valley and Hayden Valley, where wildlife roams free amid pristine backdrops. In this detailed exploration, we delve into the heart of Yellowstone's most celebrated attractions, offering practical insights, historical anecdotes, and photography tips that will enhance your adventure in America's first national park.

## Old Faithful: The Icon of Yellowstone

Few natural wonders capture the spirit of Yellowstone quite like Old Faithful. As its name implies, this geothermal marvel has earned a timeless reputation for its punctual eruptions. Rising dramatically from the park's steaming grounds, Old Faithful stands as a symbol of the raw, unbridled energy that pulses beneath Yellowstone's surface.

## The Science Behind the Spectacle

Old Faithful is a geyser that operates on a precise cycle, erupting approximately every 60 to 110 minutes. This reliable periodicity is the result of complex underground plumbing systems, where water is heated by the park's volcanic activity until it reaches a boiling point. With each eruption, water spectacularly thrusts skyward, often reaching heights between 100 to 180 feet. The geyser's impressive blasts are not only a testament to nature's power but also a vivid classroom lesson in geothermal science, offering a live demonstration of how water, heat, and pressure interact in one of the world's most dynamic thermal environments.

## Experiencing Old Faithful in Person

Visitors are encouraged to arrive early at the designated viewing areas for Old Faithful, ensuring an up-close encounter with this natural fountain. Boardwalks and observation points provide safe access to the area, allowing you to marvel at the geyser's rhythmic performance without disrupting the balance of the ecosystem. Look for informative signage and periodic ranger announcements that not only signal an impending eruption but also deliver fascinating details about the geology of the area, the history behind Old Faithful, and the practicalities of witnessing a geyser eruption.

## Photography and Observation Tips

For photography enthusiasts, capturing Old Faithful in its full glory is both a rewarding and challenging pursuit. The lighting conditions change dramatically throughout the day, from the soft hues of dawn to the vibrant colors of midday and the dramatic shadows of the evening. An early morning shoot often features a calm, misty atmosphere that enhances the ethereal quality of the geyser's plume. For those planning to use long exposure techniques, a sturdy tripod is indispensable. Experimenting with shutter speed can yield magical effects as the water transforms from a concentrated jet into a silky waterfall that appears almost otherworldly.

## Historical Context and Cultural Impact

Beyond its captivating physical nature, Old Faithful has played a pivotal role in the cultural and historical narrative of Yellowstone. Since the park's establishment in 1872, the geyser has served as a beacon for explorers, naturalists, and photographers alike. Its regular eruptions provided early visitors with a glimpse into the earth's inner workings, influencing both scientific research and public enthusiasm for preservation. Today, Old Faithful continues to inspire countless visitors who come to witness a phenomenon that feels both primal and reassuringly predictable in an ever-changing world.

# Grand Prismatic Spring: Nature's Kaleidoscope

Among the array of geothermal wonders in Yellowstone, the Grand Prismatic Spring stands out like a natural masterpiece. With its brilliant, iridescent hues and expansive size, it is a visual feast for the eyes and a challenge for even the most seasoned photographers. The spring's play of colors—from deep blues to vibrant oranges and fiery reds—creates an ever-changing canvas that epitomizes nature's artistry.

## The Geological Marvel of Grand Prismatic Spring

At nearly 370 feet in diameter, Grand Prismatic Spring is the largest hot spring in the United States. Its mesmerizing colors are the direct result of microbial mats that form around its edges. These heat-loving bacteria absorb sunlight, and their varying pigments produce the striking spectrum visible to visitors. The center of the spring is often bathed in rich, steamy blues where the temperature soars, while the outer fringes display a brilliantly luminous ring that transitions from turquoise to burnt orange. This intricate natural process not only highlights the delicate balance of Yellowstone's thermal ecosystems but also invites visitors to consider the interplay of life and environment in one of the most extreme habitats on Earth.

### Observing and Appreciating the Colors

The best vantage points for viewing Grand Prismatic Spring are the elevated boardwalks, which offer panoramic views that encompass the full scale and spectrum of the spring. As you walk along these paths, take a moment to absorb the subtle shifts in color and texture. The contrasts between the heated center and the cooler border represent more than just a visual marvel; they narrate the transformative journey of geothermal water as it moves through layers of microbial life. For many, the sight of Grand Prismatic Spring is not only mesmerizing but also spiritually uplifting —a reminder of the myriad ways life adapts and thrives.

### Tips for Photographers and Nature Lovers

When photographing the Grand Prismatic Spring, timing is everything. Early morning light, with its softer tones and lower glare, can bring out the hidden intricacies of the color gradients. Additionally, afternoon light may reveal subtle details in the surrounding landscape that add context and depth to your images. It is advisable to use polarizing filters to manage reflections from the water's surface, ensuring that the vivid colors come through crisply in your photos.

For travelers keen on a deeper exploration, guided tours offer insights into the history and science of geothermal phenomena. Park rangers and expert guides often share fascinating tidbits on how the microbial population sustains itself in extreme temperatures, adding layers of meaning to the scenic spectacle before your eyes.

### The Experience of Standing Before a Living Canvas

Grand Prismatic Spring is more than just a collection of vivid colors—it is a reminder of the dynamic processes that shape our planet. Standing before its breathtaking expanse, you may find yourself contemplating the beauty of impermanence, as the spring's colors shift with the changing light and seasons. The interplay of water, heat, and life mirrors the cycles of renewal and decay that govern every natural process.

This immersion in nature's living art form fosters a deep connection with Yellowstone's remarkable environment, encouraging an appreciation for the intricate ways in which ecosystems sustain themselves.

## Mammoth Hot Springs: A Journey Through Time

In stark contrast to the dynamic geysers and vibrant hot springs lies Mammoth Hot Springs, a landscape of terraced limestones that appears almost sculpted by human hands. These surreal, snow-white travertine terraces narrate a slow, geological tale of mineral deposition that has been unfolding for thousands of years. As water rich in dissolved limestone flows over the porous rock, it leaves behind intricate formations that shimmer under the sunlight, inviting visitors to embark on a journey through time.

### The Formation of Travertine Terraces

Mammoth Hot Springs is renowned for its extensive network of travertine terraces, which are formed by the precipitation of calcium carbonate. As hot, mineral-laden water emerges from the depths of the earth, it cascades across the surface, depositing layers of travertine that progressively build into stunning step-like formations. Over millennia, these terraces have evolved into a living record of Yellowstone's geothermal history. Walking along the well-maintained boardwalks, you can observe evidence of ancient, slow-moving water that has sculpted an otherworldly environment—a natural gallery of geological art.

### Exploring the Terraces

The area around Mammoth Hot Springs invites self-guided exploration where every twist and turn along the boardwalk reveals new perspectives and hidden patterns within the stone. Visitors can observe contrasting textures and colors—from the stark, milky white of recent deposits to the weathered, golden hues of older terraces.

Informational plaques provide insights into the processes that forge these delicate structures, bridging the gap between scientific explanation and the viewer's personal discovery.

For those with a keen interest in history, Mammoth Hot Springs also offers a glimpse into the human past. Early explorers and settlers recognized the unique qualities of the terraces, and subsequent generations have worked to preserve their beauty and ensure that their stories continue to be told. The site has long been a symbol of the park's geological treasure, inviting visitors to pause and reflect on the passage of time in a landscape defined by both change and permanence.

### Wildlife and Flora in the Surrounding Area

Despite its dry, rocky appearance, Mammoth Hot Springs is surrounded by a surprising diversity of flora and fauna. The nutrient-rich soils adjacent to the terraces support a variety of wildflowers, shrubs, and grasses that add a splash of color to the rugged terrain. Wildlife such as birds, small mammals, and even the occasional elk can be spotted meandering through the nearby meadows, providing a gentle reminder that life thrives even in the most unexpected places. This convergence of mineral landscapes and living biology reinforces the complex interplay between earth and life, making Mammoth Hot Springs a microcosm of Yellowstone's broader ecological narrative.

### Capturing the Moment

Photographers will find that Mammoth Hot Springs offers a unique set of challenges and rewards. The interplay of light and shadow against the layered terraces creates dramatic contrasts that are ideal for both wide-angle shots and detailed close-ups.

Early morning or late afternoon light, with its warm, diffused rays, can accentuate the natural contours of the travertine, revealing details that might otherwise be overlooked. Whether you are capturing the immensity of the terraces from a distance or examining the delicate textures up close, every photograph of Mammoth Hot Springs serves as a testament to the slow, relentless forces of nature.

## Yellowstone Lake: A Tranquil Waterside Retreat

At the heart of Yellowstone National Park lies Yellowstone Lake, a vast expanse of shimmering water framed by rugged mountains and dotted with verdant islands. As the park's largest body of water, Yellowstone Lake offers a peaceful counterpoint to the park's more dramatic geothermal sites, inviting visitors to linger on its shores, kayak across its gentle surface, or simply absorb the serene rhythm of nature.

### The Scenic Beauty of Yellowstone Lake

Yellowstone Lake stretches over 136 square miles, its deep blue waters reflecting the dramatic panorama of soaring ridges and dense forests. The waterfront is accessible by a network of trails and picnic areas, making it an ideal destination for families, couples, and solitude-seekers alike. The transition of the lake's color with variations in the weather—a clear blue on sunny days, shifting to milky hues during overcast skies —adds a constant element of surprise to each visit. The interplay between water and sky creates an ever-changing scene that beckons visitors to pause and appreciate the simple beauty of nature.

### Activities and Leisure by the Water

A day at Yellowstone Lake can be as active or as leisurely as you desire. For those who crave adventure, the lake is a hub for water-based activities. Kayaking, canoeing, and guided boat tours provide a unique way to experience the landscape from a different perspective. Launch points along the shoreline are conveniently located, allowing you to explore secluded coves and observe aquatic life thriving in the clear, cool waters. Anglers will delight in the varied fishing opportunities, where the tranquil environment provides an ideal backdrop for casting a line into the deep.

On quieter days, a simple lakeside picnic offers a chance to relax beneath the expansive sky. As you dine on the shores with the gentle lapping of the water in the background, pay attention to the subtle details that make this setting magical—the play of sunlight on ripples, the quiet calls of distant birds, and the delicate intermingling of water and rock along the bank. Each moment spent by Yellowstone Lake attunes you to the delicate balance between activity and peace that characterizes the natural world.

### Sunset and Photography Opportunities

Sunset over Yellowstone Lake is a sublime experience that every visitor should aspire to witness. As the sun sinks behind the distant mountains, its light casts a golden glow over the lake, transforming the water into a canvas of shimmering oranges, pinks, and purples. Photographers find these moments particularly rewarding, as the changing light creates a dynamic tableau that invites experimentation with different angles and exposures. Whether you choose to capture the scene with a wide-angle lens that includes the vast expanse of water and sky or focus in on the intricate interplay of colors along the shoreline, the resulting images will be imbued with the quiet intensity of that fleeting time of day.

### Accommodations and Visitor Facilities

The areas surrounding Yellowstone Lake offer a variety of visitor facilities, ranging from picnic areas and rest stops to educational exhibits that provide context about the lake's history and ecology. Interpretive centers near the lake offer interactive displays that detail the formation of the lake, its role in the park's ecosystem, and the cultural heritage of the region. Family-friendly programs and ranger-led tours further enrich the experience, blending leisure with learning in a way that is accessible and engaging for every age group.

## Wildlife Viewing in Lamar and Hayden Valleys

No discussion of Yellowstone's top attractions would be complete without an exploration of its world-renowned wildlife viewing areas. Among these, Lamar Valley and Hayden Valley are unrivaled in their abundance and accessibility, offering some of the best opportunities to observe the park's iconic fauna in their natural habitat.

## Lamar Valley: The Serengeti of North America

Often referred to as the "Serengeti of North America," Lamar Valley is a sprawling expanse of grassland and forest that plays host to an extraordinary variety of wildlife. This valley is a haven for large mammals such as bison, elk, wolves, and grizzly bears. Early morning drives or late afternoon visits are particularly rewarding; during these times, animals are most active, and the soft light creates a picturesque atmosphere that enhances the raw beauty of the landscape.

In Lamar Valley, the interplay between open plains and thickets of trees offers a natural stage for dramatic wildlife encounters. Bison herds roam freely across the valley floor, their slow-moving, majestic presence contrasting with the agility and keen alertness of wolves on the prowl. Observers may catch sight of predators in mid- hunt, a scene that encapsulates the timeless cycle of nature. Knowledgeable guides often point out subtle signs of animal activity—from tracks and scat to the rustle of foliage—that help to unravel the story of life in this expansive wilderness.

The valley's unobstructed vistas make it a photographer's paradise. Wide-angle lenses capture the vastness of the landscape, while telephoto lenses enable close-up shots of elusive creatures. The golden hours of early morning and late afternoon are especially magical, as the soft light bathes the valley in a warm glow that brings out the rich textures and vibrant colors of the natural habitat.

## Hayden Valley: A Window into Yellowstone's Wildlife Heartbeat

Hayden Valley, with its mirrored fields of marshland and meandering rivers, is another cornerstone of Yellowstone's wildlife viewing scene. This expansive valley is characterized by its flat, open terrain and the slow movement of the Yellowstone River, whose banks are a magnet for wildlife in search of water and lush forage. Here, visitors can often observe large herds of bison grazing against the backdrop of distant, snow-capped mountains.

The valley's serene environment is punctuated by the intermittent calls of birds and the gentle rustling of wind through tall grasses. Elk, deer, and even the occasional moose grace the meadows, their movements perfectly synchronized with the natural flow of the valley's rhythms. Perhaps the most thrilling aspect of Hayden Valley is the chance to see predators like grizzly bears moving discreetly along the river's edge, a sight that brings into focus the delicate balance of predator and prey that underpins Yellowstone's ecosystem.

For wildlife enthusiasts, Hayden Valley also provides numerous educational opportunities. Park rangers often lead guided tours in the area, explaining the ecological significance of the valley's flora and fauna. These insights, combined with personal observations of wildlife behavior, deepen one's appreciation for the intricacy and fragility of Yellowstone's ecosystem.

## Practical Wildlife Viewing Tips

Observing wildlife in Lamar and Hayden Valleys requires both patience and preparation. Always maintain a safe distance to ensure that both you and the animals remain undisturbed. Binoculars and high-quality cameras with zoom lenses are essential tools to capture these moments without intruding on the animals' natural behaviors. Early morning fog and late afternoon shadows often enhance the visual drama of the landscape, so plan your excursions around these times if your schedule allows.

Dressing in layered clothing and wearing neutral colors can help you blend into the environment, reducing the likelihood of startling wildlife. Additionally, familiarizing yourself with the park's wildlife safety guidelines is crucial—these tips not only protect you but also help preserve the natural behavior and integrity of the ecosystem.

## Insider Tips for a Memorable Encounter

While the major landmarks and wildlife valleys form the backbone of Yellowstone's allure, a few insider tips can take your visit to the next level. These suggestions are crafted to enhance your experience, ensuring that every moment in Yellowstone feels both safe and inspiring.

### Embrace the Unexpected

Nature is inherently unpredictable, and even the best-laid plans can be transformed by sudden changes in weather or unexpected wildlife encounters. Embrace the spontaneity by building flexible itineraries that allow for unplanned stops along scenic trails or at lesser-known overlooks. Sometimes the most memorable experiences come from detours that lead you to secret hot spring pools, secluded meadows, or hidden waterfalls nestled in the park's rugged terrain.

### Listen to the Stories of the Land

Every rock, geyser, and valley in Yellowstone holds a story millions of years in the making. Take the time to absorb the interpretive panels, join in ranger-led talks, or simply reflect on the raw power and beauty that surrounds you. Engaging with these narratives deepens your connection to the park, turning a visit into a journey of discovery where science, history, and art converge in the landscape itself.

### Capture More Than Just Photographs

While photographs are a wonderful way to document your adventure, consider also keeping a travel journal or sketchbook to record your impressions, thoughts, and feelings in real time. The interplay of light on a geyser's plume, the delicate shift of colors in the Grand Prismatic Spring, or the quiet majesty of a herd of bison moving across Lamar Valley are experiences that invite reflection. Jotting down your observations can help preserve the nuances of each moment, transforming fleeting impressions into lasting memories.

### Respect and Preserve the Wilderness

Yellowstone's iconic landscapes are delicate ecosystems that depend on visitors' care and respect to remain pristine for future generations. Whether you're exploring boardwalks around geothermal areas or venturing deep into wildlife valleys, adhere to the park's guidelines and Leave No Trace principles. Keeping to designated trails, packing out all your waste, and minimizing noise can help ensure that the park continues to thrive as a sanctuary for both wildlife and human wonder.

### Engage with Local Experts

Local guides and park rangers are treasure troves of information, each with intimate knowledge of Yellowstone's intricacies. They can offer recommendations on lesser- known attractions, optimal times for wildlife sightings, and hidden spots that are often missed by the casual tourist. Participating in guided tours or simply striking up a conversation with a park ranger can transform your understanding of Yellowstone, imparting insights that elevate your exploration from the ordinary to the extraordinary.

# Integrating Nature, History, and Adventure

Yellowstone National Park is a mosaic of ever-changing landscapes and timeless natural wonders that intertwine in unexpected ways. Each attraction—whether it's the explosive rhythm of Old Faithful, the painterly vibrancy of Grand Prismatic Spring, the historical allure of Mammoth Hot Springs, or the serene expanse of Yellowstone Lake and its wildlife-rich valleys—forms part of a broader narrative that speaks to the park's geological, ecological, and cultural significance.

## The Interconnected Ecosystem

Understanding one attraction within Yellowstone invariably leads you to appreciate another. The geothermal forces that give birth to Old Faithful and the Grand Prismatic Spring also influence the mineral deposits that carved Mammoth Hot Springs. The waters of Yellowstone Lake, in turn, provide sustenance to the surrounding flora and fauna, creating a seamless network of interdependent habitats. This interconnectivity is the beating heart of Yellowstone—each element is not an isolated marvel but a vital chapter in an ongoing story of natural evolution.

## Family-Friendly Exploration

For families, Yellowstone's top attractions offer a unique blend of education and excitement. Children and adults alike are drawn to the raw beauty of geysers and hot springs, the intrigue of steaming terraces, and the thrill of spotting a roaming bison herd in Lamar Valley. Many of the park's trails and viewing areas are designed with safety and accessibility in mind, making it easy for visitors of all ages to immerse themselves in nature. Interactive exhibits at visitor centers and ranger-led activities add layers of educational value while keeping the sense of wonder alive, inviting each family member to discover Yellowstone in their own way.

## Seasonal Splendors

The seasonal transformations of Yellowstone are as much an attraction as the landmarks themselves. In spring, the awakening of flora and fauna, coupled with a light dusting of snow on high ridges, sets a gentle, hopeful tone. Summer brings long, sunlit days that allow for extensive exploration, while the autumn months dress the park in a tapestry of rich, warm colors. Even winter, with its blanket of snow and steaming geothermal features that stand out against the cold, offers a dramatic and introspective experience. Visitors who plan their adventures around these seasonal shifts will find that Yellowstone never ceases to reinvent its splendor.

## Preparing for Diverse Experiences

Yellowstone's vast wilderness demands a thoughtful approach to exploration. Weather can shift unexpectedly, and the terrain ranges dramatically from flat valley floors to uneven geothermal areas. Pack suitable clothing, sturdy hiking boots, and always carry water and snacks in your daypack. Each attraction often comes with specific safety guidelines—especially around thermal features, where the ground may be fragile and the water scalding. Familiarize yourself with these tips and advice provided throughout the park to maximize both your enjoyment and safety.

## The Legacy of Yellowstone's Iconic Spots

The iconic attractions in Yellowstone are not only beautiful landmarks; they are living legacies that have shaped and been shaped by the park's stewardship over the decades. Conservation efforts, guided by robust scientific research and an enduring commitment to environmental ethics, help ensure that these wonders remain largely untouched by the pressures of modern development. By following park regulations and cherishing the quiet dignity of Yellowstone's singular landscapes, each visitor contributes to a legacy of preservation that is as enduring as the land itself.

Every observation, every photo, and every quiet moment taken along a steaming geyser or a mirror-like lake ripples outward into a collective memory that honors the timeless wonder of Yellowstone National Park. Whether it is the rhythmic pulse of Old Faithful reminding you of the power of nature, the kaleidoscopic display of Grand Prismatic Spring offering a glimpse into a microbial world far beyond ordinary perception, or the gentle progression of travertine terraces at Mammoth Hot Springs that whisper stories of Earth's ancient past—each attraction encapsulates a distinct facet of Yellowstone's multifaceted beauty.

Immersed in these natural features, visitors come to understand that Yellowstone is not merely a destination, but an expansive, living narrative. Every pathway, every vista, and every encounter weaves together to form an experience that is as enriching as it is exhilarating. From the well-worn trails of Mammoth Hot Springs to the uncharted ways of Lamar and Hayden Valleys, each step taken in this vibrant landscape deepens one's connection to the land, its history, and its enduring promise of discovery.

The extraordinary confluence of geothermal marvels, rugged wilderness, and dynamic ecosystems that defines Yellowstone's top attractions fuels both a spirit of adventure and a reverence for the natural world. With each new discovery along the trail, every visitor is invited to participate in a timeless dialogue with nature—a conversation that spans millions of years and continues to evolve with every sunlit day and starlit night in Yellowstone.

Whether you are embarking on your first journey through these storied landscapes or returning with fresh eyes to witness the park's perennial wonders, Yellowstone's must-see spots offer compelling reasons to slow down, look closely, and savor each unparalleled moment in time. The interplay of dynamic geology, vibrant life, and ever-changing light ensures that every visit leaves an indelible impression—one that beckons you to return, to explore further, and to let the magic of Yellowstone continue its silent conversation with your soul.

By carefully weaving together iconic landmarks, captivating geological wonders, and world-class wildlife viewing opportunities, Yellowstone stands as a testament to nature's ability to inspire awe and wonder. Each highlighted attraction serves as a vivid chapter in a grand narrative where science, beauty, and the enduring spirit of the wild come together in harmonious celebration. Let your journey through Yellowstone be guided by these treasures, and you will discover a profound appreciation for the majestic, interconnected tapestry that defines this national park.

As you explore these attractions, allow yourself the freedom to wander, to pause, and to absorb each visual and emotional detail that Yellowstone offers. Whether your focus is on the reliability of Old Faithful, the mesmerizing palette of Grand Prismatic Spring, the timeless elegance of Mammoth Hot Springs, or the quiet yet thrilling calls of wildlife in Lamar and Hayden Valleys, every encounter is an invitation to experience the grand narrative of nature as it unfolds around you.

# SCENIC DRIVES & HIKING TRAILS

## Scenic Drives & Hiking Trails in Yellowstone National Park

Yellowstone National Park is a living mosaic of dramatic landscapes, steaming geysers, vibrant hot springs, and serene backcountry trails that invite every traveler to experience nature at its most elemental. Whether you're winding along paved park roads or hiking rugged back trails through primeval forests and steaming thermal areas, the journey through Yellowstone is as much about the road and the path as it is about the ultimate destination. This section details some of the park's most picturesque drives and hiking trails, offering guidance on what to expect, how to prepare, and where to find those hidden gems that make every visit a unique adventure.

## Exploring the Scenic Drives

### The Grand Loop Road: The Beating Heart of Yellowstone

The Grand Loop Road serves as the central artery of Yellowstone National Park, branching out to the park's most iconic attractions and serving as the gateway to nature's wonders. Stretching in a rough figure-eight pattern throughout the park, this winding route is highly accessible for families and solo adventurers alike.

Driving along the Grand Loop Road, you'll pass by sprawling meadows dotted with grazing bison, dramatic canyons carved by ancient rivers, and thermal areas where the earth gives off its secrets. The drive itself is visually arresting, with constantly changing scenery that reflects Yellowstone's rich geologic history and its active geothermal features.

Because traffic on this loop can be significant during the summer months, planning a drive during early morning or late afternoon hours can help you avoid crowds. Along the way, regular pull-offs and designated viewpoints offer opportunities to safely capture photographs, stretch your legs, and soak in panoramic views. Keep a close eye out for park signage that details geological formations and the park's wildlife patterns.

Families will appreciate the accessibility of the Grand Loop Road. Many segments are paved and well-maintained, ensuring that even those with mobility challenges can enjoy the drive. Several shorter, easily accessible trailheads branch off this road, making it ideal for a combination of short hikes and scenic drives all in one day. Informative roadside markers explain the natural history behind the geysers and hot springs, adding depth to your journey and enriching the overall experience.

## The Firehole Canyon Drive and Geyser Basins

Another scenic drive that promises a mix of adventure and education is the route leading to the Firehole Canyon area and the park's impressive geyser basins. This drive takes you through narrow canyons bordered by rugged rock formations and provides close-up views of the thermal activity that characterizes much of Yellowstone's landscape. Before reaching the canyon, the road meanders past boiling pools, vibrant hot springs, and steaming vents that can be safely admired from a distance.

Firehole Canyon Drive is especially appealing for those interested in the scientific and historical aspects of Yellowstone. As you drive, interpretative signs offer insights into the park's geothermal processes, and knowledgeable rangers provide context for the visible eruptions that tell a tale of the restless earth beneath. The route is moderately easy, with sections that require a cautious approach due to sharp curves and narrow passages. It is advisable to check road conditions and closures, especially in the shoulder seasons when wildlife crossings are more frequent.

This drive also leads into areas from which several excellent hiking trails begin. One popular starting point is near the Firehole Lake Drive, where short walks allow you to edge closer to dramatic thermal vistas and learn about the interplay between water and heat that creates Yellowstone's famous features. Whether you are interested in the geology, botany, or the photographic opportunities provided by the interplay of light and steam, Firehole Canyon Drive offers something memorable at each bend.

## Lamar Valley Scenic Byway: Wildlife and Unspoiled Beauty

Few drives in Yellowstone compare to the Lamar Valley Scenic Byway, a route celebrated by photographers and wildlife enthusiasts alike. Known as the "Serengeti of North America," Lamar Valley is one of the best places in the park to observe large herds of bison, elk, and occasionally wolves in their natural environment. The vast open spaces, rolling hills, and meandering rivers create the perfect stage for watching nature unfold in slow motion.

Driving slowly through Lamar Valley allows you to witness the subtleties of the landscape, where every turn may reveal a scene that seems lifted from a National Geographic spread. The valley is particularly captivating in the early morning or late afternoon, when the low light accentuates the textures of the land and the subtle movements of its inhabitants.

For families, the Lamar Valley Scenic Byway can be a moving classroom in natural history. The expansive views invite passengers of all ages to observe earth's ecology and understand the relationships between predators and prey. Informative rest stops and natural history exhibits scattered along the route further enrich your knowledge of the region's biological diversity. Travelers should remain patient and respectful, using binoculars and keeping a safe distance to avoid disturbing the wildlife in this delicate ecosystem.

### Hidden Roads: Discovering the Lesser-Known Routes

While the main routes through Yellowstone offer plenty of opportunities for exploration, a sense of adventure calls to many who wish to delve off the beaten path. Several lesser-known roads and gravel tracks lie hidden deep within the park, accessible to those with a spirit of exploration and a four-wheel-drive vehicle. These hidden roads wind through backcountry forests, past isolated geothermal features, and along mountain ridges that offer an intimate encounter with Yellowstone's raw wilderness.

One particularly enchanting drive begins near the edge of the park's central zone and meanders into a forest of lodgepole pine, where sunlight filters through in dappled patterns on the forest floor. This route, while unofficial in parts, is marked by a series of natural clearings and small, secluded overlooks, each providing an opportunity for quiet reflection and excellent photo opportunities. Travelers are advised to exercise caution, adhere to park regulations, and consult park maps because these off-the- beaten-path routes are often less maintained and may present challenges not found on well-traveled roads.

Each hidden road carries its own set of surprises—an unexpected herd of deer crossing at dusk, a bubbling spring tucked away in a shaded grove, or an overlook that commands a staggering view of Yellowstone Lake. For those equipped with proper navigation tools and a sense of adventure, these hidden drives offer some of the most intimate experiences the park has to offer. Moreover, they provide direct access to several trailheads that lead into untouched backcountry areas where the natural world unfolds in ways that remind you of Yellowstone's timeless magic.

## Hiking Trails: On Foot Through Yellowstone's Wonders

### Getting Started with Yellowstone's Hiking Trails

Yellowstone's hiking trails provide direct contact with nature, from the thermal wonders hidden among rocky outcrops to the sweeping vistas along mountain passes. The park is designed to accommodate hikers of all abilities, featuring an array of trails from easy, family-friendly walks to challenging backcountry treks. Each trail offers its own blend of unique geological phenomena, wildlife sightings, and breathtaking scenery.

Before you set out, it's essential to prepare appropriately. Always check current trail conditions at visitor centers or online, pack sufficient water, and dress in layers to accommodate sudden changes in weather. Along popular trails, well-maintained boardwalks and signposts help guide visitors safely past geothermal hazards, while more rugged paths require careful navigation and a heightened awareness of your surroundings. Having a trail map and a basic understanding of the park's layout will greatly enhance your hiking experience.

Respect for the natural environment is paramount. Always adhere to Leave No Trace principles by staying on designated paths, packing out all waste, and minimizing impact on the delicate ecosystems you traverse. Yellowstone's trails are living specimens of natural history, and preserving them is essential to ensuring that future generations can enjoy the same splendors.

### The Iconic Mount Washburn Trail

Among the park's most famous hikes, the Mount Washburn Trail stands out for its panoramic views and relative accessibility. Starting from the Chittenden Road area in the northeastern section of the park, this trail provides hikers with a rewarding climb that culminates in breathtaking vistas stretching across Yellowstone's diverse landscapes.

The trail is moderately strenuous, making it suitable for families with active teens and adventurous solo hikers alike. The climb is steady, with switchbacks that gradually increase your elevation and offer intermittent views of the surrounding valleys and distant mountains. As you ascend, the vegetation changes from dense pine forests to sparse alpine tundra, reflecting the transition from lower to higher altitudes. In the summer, wildflowers punctuate the rocky slopes with bursts of color against the rugged landscape.

At the summit, the expansive view is nothing short of sensational. On clear days, you can see several of Yellowstone's major landmarks, including the colorful Grand Prismatic Spring in the distance, as well as glimpses of the surrounding mountain ranges that define the park's skyline. This trail also serves as an excellent opportunity for wildlife viewing, especially in the early morning or late afternoon when deer and marmots are often more active. Interpretative markers along the trail explain the geology and ecology of the area, enriching your understanding of the forces that have shaped this unique environment.

### The Fairy Falls and Imperial Geyser Loop

Another must-explore hiking option is the loop that combines the enchanting Fairy Falls Trail with the nearby Imperial Geyser area. This trail provides an immersive experience that blends a gentle, scenic hike with an up-close view of Yellowstone's dynamic geothermal features.

Beginning at a well-marked parking area near the Midway Geyser Basin, the Fairy Falls Trail takes you past a series of verdant meadows and trickling streams before opening out to reveal the majestic Fairy Falls—a cascade of water that tumbles over rocky ledges amid a backdrop of lush foliage. The sound of water and the cool mist from the falls create a sensory haven that invites you to pause and absorb the natural beauty of your surroundings.

Continuing along the loop, the path directs you to the Imperial Geyser, one of Yellowstone's lesser-known yet captivating geothermal features. As you approach, the ground beneath your feet may seem to shimmer with heat, a tangible reminder of the subterranean activity at work. Along this part of the hike, geological interpretative panels offer context on the park's complex hydrothermal systems, explaining how water, heat, and silica interact to produce such mesmerizing displays. The loop not only makes for a comfortable day hike but also enriches your understanding of the natural processes that make Yellowstone one of the world's most geologically active landscapes.

This trail is particularly appealing to families, as its moderate difficulty and abundance of scenic spots keep younger hikers engaged. Early in the season, the bright colors of new foliage and the gentle sounds of wildlife create a peaceful, almost storybook-like atmosphere. Hikers are encouraged to take frequent breaks, enjoy a picnic in one of the designated areas, and reflect on how the interplay between water, steam, and rock has sculpted one of the park's most endearing attractions.

### Lone Star Geyser Trail: A Short But Engaging Expedition

For those seeking a shorter excursion that still packs a punch in terms of geological wonder, the Lone Star Geyser Trail is an excellent choice. This easy to moderate hike is ideal for visitors who want to experience the soothing sights and sounds of Yellowstone's geyser basins without committing to a long trek.

The trail winds gently through a mixed landscape of open meadows, scattered trees, and clusters of thermal features. Along the route, interpretative signage provides key insights into the science behind geyser eruptions and hot spring formations. The highlight of the trail is, naturally, the Lone Star Geyser—a frequently erupting feature that delights with its predictable bursts of steaming water and rhythmic splashes. The geyser's periodic displays offer a natural "clockwork" that can be mesmerizing to watch, especially for children who are fascinated by the timing and energy behind each eruption.

Despite its shorter length, the Lone Star Geyser Trail manages to capture the essential spirit of Yellowstone's geothermal activity. The path is well-maintained and offers several points where hikers can safely step off the main trail to examine ice formations in the winter months or clusters of wildflowers in the summer. Given its relatively flat grade, this trail is accessible to families with strollers, making it another favorite among visitors looking for a manageable, yet engaging, hike.

## Off-the-Beaten-Path Trails: Discovering Yellowstone's Hidden Gems

Beyond the well-trodden favorite trails, Yellowstone is crisscrossed with lesser-known tracks that provide solitude and an up-close encounter with its most pristine natural settings. These off-the-beaten-path trails are intended for those who appreciate quiet exploration and have gained some experience trekking in the wild. They often demand a higher level of preparedness, as the terrain may be uneven, and emergency services might be sparse.

One such hidden trail leads into the remote reaches of the park's backcountry near the West Thumb Geyser Basin. This trail, often bypassed by large groups, offers hikers a chance to experience the raw beauty of Yellowstone's lakeside ecosystems. The route meanders along the shores of Yellowstone Lake, where the interplay of light on water creates shimmering reflections of rugged mountains and distant forests. Along the way, you may encounter secluded hot springs tucked into coves, igniting the sense that every step holds an undiscovered secret.

The off-the-beaten-path trails are typically marked with less frequent signage, encouraging hikers to rely on detailed maps and a sense of adventure. These routes, while more challenging, are incredibly rewarding. In addition to unspoiled landscapes and opportunities for quiet wildlife observation, these trails often lead to vantage points that few visitors ever see, such as hidden drop-offs over cascading waterfalls or secret clearings that offer uninterrupted views of the park's towering peaks. Hikers who venture on these less-traveled paths are advised to inform park rangers of their itinerary, carry a satellite or emergency beacon if possible, and always practice strict Leave No Trace policies to preserve these pristine areas.

## The Continental Divide Trail in Yellowstone

An extension of Yellowstone's hiking repertoire is the segment of the Continental Divide Trail that crosses parts of the park. This famous trail, which spans the North American continent, offers an adventurous opportunity for those looking to integrate a piece of a transcontinental journey into their Yellowstone experience. Within the park boundaries, the trail meanders through rugged canyons and leads to panoramic overlooks that illustrate why Yellowstone remains a magnet for hikers from around the world.

The section of the Continental Divide Trail in Yellowstone is considered more challenging due to its steeper ascents and descents, variable weather conditions, and occasional rocky terrain. However, the trail is also one of the most rewarding, as it connects you to the ancient geological history of the continent. As you hike this rugged section, interpretive markers explain the significance of the divide – a natural boundary where water flows in opposite directions, contributing to the park's unique hydrology and ecological diversity.

Hikers on this segment are often treated to extraordinary encounters with Yellowstone's quieter wildlife scenes. The quiet solitude of the Continental Divide section, combined with the panoramic views from its higher elevations, provides an invigorating escape from the more crowded park areas. Prepared hikers bring detailed topographic maps and adequate supplies, and many find that a multi-day trek along this segment creates memories that last a lifetime.

### Exploring Loop Trails and Family-Friendly Routes

Yellowstone also offers numerous loop trails that are specifically designed for ease of access and brief, yet highly scenic, excursions. These loops are ideal for families who wish for short outdoor adventures or for visitors who have limited time but still want to experience the park's natural joy. Often beginning and ending at the same accessible trailhead, these loops are well-marked and typically feature interpretative displays along the way.

One such loop is the Blacktail Plateau Drive, which, despite being classified as a scenic drive, incorporates several short walking trails along its route. The Blacktail Plateau connects different habitats—transitioning from dense forest to open meadows—and provides a rich tapestry of natural history. Along this drive, small trail branches allow hikers to step off the main road to examine local vegetation, observe bird life, and even enjoy a brief picnic in one of the park's designated rest areas. The friendly, open-air nature of these loop trails ensures that hikers of all ages find them manageable and enjoyable, and many families weave these loops into their daily itineraries to intersperse moments of quiet reflection amidst the park's more energetic attractions.

## Practical Information for Scenic Drives and Hiking Trails

### Trail Difficulty and Safety Tips

Yellowstone's trails vary widely in difficulty, ranging from gentle boardwalk strolls to strenuous climbs that challenge even seasoned hikers. It is crucial to assess your own fitness level, plan according to the weather conditions, and be aware of your surroundings.

- Always start your hikes from designated trailheads, where you can find updated information on path conditions and potential hazards.

- Wear sturdy hiking boots, dress in layers to adjust to rapidly changing mountain weather, and carry a basic first aid kit.

- Wildlife, such as bears and elk, is often encountered along these routes. It is advisable to travel in groups where possible and carry bear spray, especially on more remote trails.

- Keep to established paths and boardwalks in geothermal areas to avoid dangerous, unstable ground or superheated surfaces.

- Silence your devices or use discretion when capturing photos to avoid startling wildlife or disturbing other trail users.

These precautions ensure that both the majesty of Yellowstone and your personal safety are preserved, allowing you to fully immerse yourself in the experience without undue risk.

## Accessibility and Seasonal Considerations

Yellowstone's accessibility varies significantly with the seasons. In the summer, most major trails and drives are open and well-maintained, though popularity can mean more crowded conditions. Early mornings or weekdays are ideal if you prefer a quieter experience.

During the fall and early spring, some roads and trails may be closed due to snow or inclement weather. In these shoulder seasons, portions of the park offer a different perspective—tranquil, with frost-tipped meadows and fewer visitors—but require greater preparation in terms of warm clothing, additional food and water, and sometimes specialized equipment like crampons or trekking poles.

For travelers with mobility issues or families with small children, Yellowstone provides several paved boardwalks and short, interpretative trails that are both safe and engaging. Many viewpoints along scenic drives come equipped with benches and accessible pathways, ensuring that everyone, regardless of physical ability, has the opportunity to experience the park's unrivaled beauty.

## Duration and Itinerary Planning

The duration of your scenic drives and hiking excursions can range from a couple of hours to full-day adventures, depending on your interests and physical ability. A typical itinerary might include a relaxed morning drive along the Grand Loop Road, followed by a couple of short hikes to nearby thermal features and viewpoints, with time allocated for leisurely breaks to observe wildlife or sketch the landscape.

For those planning a multi-day trip, consider designing a flexible itinerary that intersperses longer hikes, such as a full-day adventure on the Mount Washburn Trail or a segment of the Continental Divide Trail, with restorative scenic drives that allow you to experience Yellowstone at a more languid pace. This approach not only prevents exhaustion but also provides more opportunities to appreciate the nuances of the park's changing environment.

## Gear Checklist for Drivers and Hikers

To fully enjoy Yellowstone's scenic drives and hiking trails, preparation is key. A well-thought-out gear checklist might include:

**For drivers:** - Detailed park maps (both physical and digital) - A reliable vehicle with adequate fuel, especially in remote areas - Emergency supplies, including water, food, and a basic first aid kit - Binoculars and a camera with extra batteries or power banks for wildlife photography - Navigation apps or GPS devices with the latest updates on trail closures and road conditions

**For hikers:** - Sturdy, waterproof footwear and layered clothing suitable for unpredictable weather - Ample water, snacks, and possibly a portable stove for longer treks - Sunscreen, insect repellent, and a hat for sun protection at higher altitudes - A backpack equipped with a first aid kit, map, compass, and possibly a whistle for emergencies - Lightweight rain gear that can be easily stowed in your pack Ensuring you have these essentials not only enhances safety but also maximizes your enjoyment by allowing you to focus on the natural splendor unfolding before you.

# Experiencing the Intersection of Scenic Drives and Hiking Trails

## Combining Your Road Trip with On-Foot Exploration

One of the most rewarding ways to experience Yellowstone is to blend your scenic drive with carefully chosen hiking detours. The park's layout is such that major scenic drives naturally lead to trailheads, giving you the freedom to decide whether to simply savor the view from your vehicle or to pause and embark on a more intimate exploration on foot.

For example, a day dedicated to driving through Lamar Valley can be interspersed with short stops to trek along small loop trails that lead to excellent wildlife viewing spots. From the comfort of your car, you might enjoy panoramic vistas and then disembark at a secluded overlook where a short, interpretative walking trail provides deeper insight into the surrounding terrain and its inhabitants. Alternating between the relaxation of a scenic drive and the physical engagement of a hike creates a balanced itinerary that caters to diverse interests and energy levels.

Another popular combination involves using the Grand Loop Road as a backbone, with scheduled stops at key trailheads such as those for Mount Washburn or the Fairy Falls Loop. This approach lets you control the pace of your adventure and customize your route based on real-time conditions such as weather, wildlife activity, and your personal levels of excitement and endurance.

## Engaging With Nature Along the Way

Each scenic drive and trail in Yellowstone offers a dynamic classroom of natural wonders. As you traverse elevated highways or cross tumbling streams on hidden trails, visitors are invited to observe a range of natural phenomena—from the subtle play of light on distant peaks to the rhythmic pulse of thermal eruptions.

On many drives, interpretation signs invite you to read about the unique chemical compositions of the hot springs or the recurring patterns of geyser eruptions. These informational panels help contextualize what might initially appear as overwhelming visual spectacles. Similarly, while hiking, every bend in the path might reveal a burst of wildflowers, the tracks of a deer in fresh snow, or the curious behavior of a marmot emerging from its burrow. Attentive observation harmonizes beautifully with spontaneous exploration, turning each moment into an opportunity to deepen your understanding of Yellowstone's ecological tapestry.

The park's scenic drives also encourage moments of spontaneous reflection. When the road opens up to an uninterrupted vista of expansive meadows or a distant mountain range, there is both a literal and figurative moment to pause. This is not just a travel itinerary but an immersive, meditative engagement with nature that deepens the appreciation for the conservation values that Yellowstone embodies. Such experiences forge lasting memories and connections, reminding visitors that the true journey is as much internal as it is external.

## Seasonal Variations and Photographic Opportunities

As the seasons change, so too does the visual narrative of Yellowstone. In the early summer, fresh green leaves and bursts of colorful wildflowers contrast with the rugged, weathered rocks, providing an almost impressionistic quality to the scenery. Late summer and early fall add warm hues to the landscape—with golden aspens, deep red rock formations, and the gentle mist that often shrouds the geyser basins at dawn. Winter transforms the park into a serene snowscape, where the silence is occasionally broken by the disturbed patter of wildlife moving cautiously across the frozen ground.

These seasonal transformations offer distinct photographic opportunities for every keen observer. Photography enthusiasts can take advantage of the soft morning light during the quieter seasons of early spring and late fall, or the stark contrasts of sunlight and shadow common during peak summer hours. Many scenic drives include stops that are ideal for capturing wide-angle shots, while the trails lend themselves to more intimate, detailed compositions. Whether you are a casual smartphone photographer or a seasoned DSLR user, every angle of Yellowstone— whether viewed from the window of your car or from the rugged trail—offers a frame-worthy postcard moment.

## Customizing Your Yellowstone Experience

No two visits to Yellowstone are the same, and the combination of scenic drives with hiking trails offers a highly customizable experience. If you prefer a leisurely pace, consider carving out a day for uninterrupted road trips, allowing you to linger at viewpoints and take detours into smaller trails. On other days, especially if you're feeling energetic, plan for longer hikes that lead you into the deeper recesses of the park's more remote corners.

For families, a well-structured itinerary could involve a morning drive along one of the major scenic routes with multiple stops, interlaced with short hikes that active children and seniors alike can enjoy. Alternately, a multi-day excursion might incorporate overnight camping at designated sites accessible by both car and foot, ensuring that every segment of the adventure—from scenic drives to mountainous trails—is encountered with both safety and a sense of discovery.

Each experience in Yellowstone is enriched by personal considerations such as fitness level, interests in wildlife or geology, and the pace at which you prefer to explore. By blending time on the road with well-planned hikes, you can create a tapestry of memories that encompass the full spectrum of Yellowstone's wonders—from the grand vistas of its highways to the quiet, introspective corridors of its hiking trails.

## Navigational Tools and Digital Aids

In this modern age of technology, numerous digital aids have arrived to help guide your journey through Yellowstone's extensive network of roads and trails.

Smartphone applications specifically designed for national parks offer interactive maps that detail trail difficulties, real-time updates on road conditions, and user- generated tips on the best viewpoints and photo stops.

Many visitors find that downloading a few key apps before embarking on their adventure significantly enhances the experience. Not only can these apps help you avoid potential hazards by alerting you to unexpected closures or severe weather, but they also provide curated itineraries and suggestions based on your interests.

Whether it's identifying that hidden loop trail near Firehole Canyon or finding the most accessible viewpoint in Lamar Valley, digital navigation transforms every drive and hike into a seamlessly integrated adventure.

When using these tools, it's important to remember that service in remote areas may be limited. Carrying a paper map as a backup, along with ensuring your devices are charged and equipped with portable power sources, is always a wise precaution.

Leveraging both modern technology and traditional navigational wisdom ensures that your journey remains both safe and brilliantly enigmatic.

## Unique Challenges and Rewards of Yellowstone's Terrain

Yellowstone's dynamic natural environment means that every journey carries with it a blend of unpredictability and reward. The park's volcanic history and ongoing geothermal activity shape an ever-changing landscape where new phenomena can appear with little warning. This means that even familiar routes may occasionally present unexpected views—a previously dormant hot spring might begin to steam, or a well-known trail could reveal a newly defined path through thickening underbrush.

For the experienced traveler, these nuances of Yellowstone's terrain are part of the enduring charm of the park. The interplay between natural hazards and sublime beauty calls for a mindful and respectful approach. Always check with park rangers for any recent changes in trail or road conditions, carry updated local guides, and be ready to adapt your itinerary. This sense of living on the edge of a dynamic, living ecosystem contributes to the authenticity and unpredictability that have defined Yellowstone as a destination for adventurers for over a century.

In many ways, the challenges inherent in Yellowstone's landscape are matched by its rewards. The steep ascent of a mountain trail might be taxing, but every drop of sweat is repaid with a vista so breathtaking it transcends the effort. Whether it's the quiet majesty of a secluded canyon discovered through an uncharted trail or the joyful chorus of wildlife witnessed along a scenic drive, the park demands both preparation and humility. In return, it offers moments of transcendence—a shared silence with nature and a reminder of the power of the natural world.

## Integrating Storytelling with Exploration

The narrative of Yellowstone isn't confined to guidebooks and trail markers—it unfolds with every step you take along a winding path or every mile crisscrossed on a scenic drive. Listening to the stories of early explorers, indigenous peoples, and modern park rangers enriches every segment of your journey. As you drive along the Grand Loop Road or hike toward an ancient geothermal trail, take time to ponder not just what you see, but also the historical and cultural context behind these marvels.

Many interpretative signs and ranger-led talks provide vivid accounts of the natural forces that have sculpted Yellowstone over millennia. Incorporating these narratives deepens your connection with the landscape. You start to appreciate Yellowstone not only for its visual splendor but also for its role in the larger story of America's natural and cultural heritage. The combination of manual exploration and historical storytelling makes every scenic drive and hiking trail a chapter in a grand, unfolding epic of nature and time.

## Making the Most of Your Visit

Planning for a visit that includes both scenic drives and hiking trails requires thoughtful scheduling and an adaptive mindset. Carefully consider the time of day, park traffic, and seasonal shifts when designing your itinerary. Balancing periods of introspection with bursts of activity will ensure that you experience Yellowstone's beauty without feeling rushed.

Before setting off on any trail, take time to study the local weather forecasts, consult with park rangers, and share your plans with someone outside the park. These steps are particularly important if you plan to explore areas that are less frequented or if you intend to hike longer distances where fewer resources are available. By staying informed and being flexible, you guarantee that every minute spent in the park is optimally safe and exceptionally rewarding.

Many experienced visitors find that maintaining a travel journal or a nature sketchbook can add an extra dimension to the journey. Not only does it serve as a personal memoir of the sights and experiences encountered on various drives and trails, but it also helps you notice the subtle changes in nature—from the shift of light in the early morning to the patterns of wildlife behavior at dusk. These reflective activities can elevate your trip from a mere observational tour to a profound, reflective experience in nature.

## Concluding With Lasting Impressions

Yellowstone National Park's scenic drives and hiking trails encapsulate the essence of the park—a seamless blend of geologic dynamism, abundant wildlife, and serene, soul-stirring vistas. Each drive and hike is designed to connect you more deeply with the earth's natural rhythms, revealing the evolving narrative of a landscape that has captivated explorers for generations.

Whether you follow the well-traveled paths of the Grand Loop Road, explore the wildlife-rich plains of Lamar Valley, or venture onto the less charted trails near the West Thumb Geyser Basin, every turn offers a glimpse into the enduring magic of Yellowstone. From the accessible, family-friendly routes accompanied by educational signage, to the more challenging trails that require careful preparation and a spirit of adventure, the array of options ensures that every visitor finds something that resonates with their personal sense of wonder.

As you navigate these scenic drives and hiking trails, you embark on an intimate dialogue with nature—a conversation punctuated by the sounds of rushing water, the calls of distant wildlife, and the soft rustle of aspen leaves against a backdrop of ancient rock. Here in Yellowstone, the journey is as important as the destination, and each moment along the road or on the trail is woven into the larger tapestry of natural grandeur.

Armed with detailed maps, trustworthy digital navigation aids, and a respect for the delicate balance of this extraordinary environment, your exploration becomes an act of stewardship as well as adventure. Every mile traveled and every footstep taken contributes to an understanding of how deeply connected we all are to the natural world—a realization as timeless as the park's own geological history.

Yellowstone invites you to step away from the ordinary and into a realm where every scenic drive and hiking trail offers a portal to awe-inspiring beauty and dynamic natural history. In this vast and ever-changing landscape, the journey is a constant reminder of nature's boundless creativity and resilience—a treasure trove waiting to be discovered, explored, and cherished time and time again.

# CAMPING & ACCOMMODATIONS

## Exploring Camping & Accommodations in Yellowstone

Yellowstone National Park offers a wide range of camping and accommodation options that cater to every traveler's needs—from rugged tent sites nestled in the wild to historic lodges exuding the charm of yesteryear. Whether you are a solo adventurer, a family seeking outdoor adventures, or an RV enthusiast ready to hit the open road, Yellowstone provides carefully maintained spots and unique lodging experiences crafted to enhance your enjoyment and interaction with nature. With its diverse ecosystems and breathtaking landscapes, the park promises not only a place to set up camp but also an immersive experience that deepens your connection to one of America's most storied national treasures.

## Campgrounds: The Traditional Yellowstone Camping Experience

Yellowstone National Park hosts several established campgrounds that offer comfortable settings for pitching your tent or parking your RV. These campgrounds vary in size, amenities, and location, allowing visitors to choose a site that best suits their travel style.

Many of the park's campgrounds are strategically located so that campers are never far from iconic attractions. For example, **Madison Campground** sits near both the Madison River and several geothermal features, making it ideal for those who wish to mix camping with easy access to Yellowstone's geysers and hot springs. The campground's layout provides ample space between sites, making it a popular choice for visitors who appreciate a balance between solitude and opportunity for meeting fellow campers.

Equally popular is **Canyon Campground**, located near the dramatic Grand Canyon of the Yellowstone. Its proximity to striking waterfalls and scenic vistas makes it a magnet for photographers and adventurers keen to explore the rugged beauty of Yellowstone's terrain. You'll find that each site is designed with practicality in mind, with clearly marked fire rings, picnic tables, and nearby restroom facilities that add a layer of comfort without detracting from the natural surroundings.

Another notable campground is **Grant Village Campground**, offering a serene environment close to the shores of Yellowstone Lake. The calm waters and sweeping vistas provide a peaceful backdrop for those looking to relax after a long day exploring the park. Visitors here benefit from easy access to water-based activities such as fishing or canoeing, making Grant Village a well-rounded base for outdoor recreation.

Yellowstone's campgrounds are not only about shelter and sleep; they are hubs of community activity and storytelling. Evenings by the campfire often turn into lively gatherings where seasoned explorers exchange tips on the best wildlife viewing spots or share tales of past adventures. For first-time visitors, these interactions can be a valuable source of insider knowledge, inspiring confidence and anticipation for the days ahead.

## RV Camping: Navigating the Roads with Comfort and Convenience

For those traveling with an RV, Yellowstone National Park is a destination that provides modern conveniences within a remarkably wild setting. RV campers will find that several campgrounds offer electrical hookups, dump stations, and water facilities designed to make life on the road as comfortable as possible while still preserving the park's natural allure.

Campgrounds such as the ones mentioned earlier are well-equipped to handle RVs, though it is important to note that space can be at a premium during peak travel seasons. Because of this, reserving a spot well in advance is highly recommended.

Many sites implement seasonal booking systems that require early planning, often many months ahead of the camping season, to ensure both availability and a spot that fits your specific needs.

It is essential for RV travelers to be aware of the park's size restrictions and road regulations designed to minimize environmental impact. While many modern RV parks offer full hookups, Yellowstone's campgrounds are more rustic and offer only limited facilities, designed to blend into the natural surroundings without detracting from the wilderness experience. Preparation is key: make sure your RV's systems are in good working order, and pack additional supplies for extended stays, as resupply options within the park can be limited.

For those who might be traveling with larger RVs or trailers, it can be beneficial to confirm site measurements ahead of time. Some campgrounds have size limitations that might restrict access for oversized vehicles, so checking available details on the official park website or contacting the campground management can save time and avoid disappointment. Taking the time to review campsite ratings and visitor feedback can also provide insights into terrain conditions, parking convenience, and overall accessibility. Moreover, using designated dumping stations and following the park's waste disposal guidelines ensures that you contribute to the preservation of the majestic landscape and maintain the pristine quality of Yellowstone's environment.

## Lodges: Experiencing the Comforts of Historic Charm

Beyond the traditional campgrounds, Yellowstone is home to a collection of charming lodges that bring a touch of historical elegance to the rugged park setting. The lodges provide an excellent alternative for those who prefer a bit more comfort without sacrificing the park's incomparable views and natural beauty.

Among the most famous is the **Old Faithful Inn**, a National Historic Landmark known for its rustic architecture, massive stone fireplaces, and sweeping log and timber accents. Staying at Old Faithful Inn not only offers visitors a front-row seat to the park's geothermal wonders but also a glimpse into a rich heritage that dates back to the park's early days. The Inn's robust construction and unique design allow guests to feel as though they are part of Yellowstone's living history, an experience that combines luxury with the raw elements of nature.

Another jewel in Yellowstone's lodging crown is the **Lake Yellowstone Hotel & Cabins**. With its timeless elegance and sophisticated decor, the hotel overlooks the serene waters of Yellowstone Lake. The sound of lapping waves and the panoramic view of the surrounding mountains create an atmosphere of calm that is perfect for relaxation after a day of exploration. Guests can enjoy a variety of amenities including fine dining, guided tours, and seasonal activities that make this historic establishment a versatile choice for any visitor.

Additional lodging options on park property provide a range of choices from cozy cabins to modern hotel rooms. These accommodations vary in price and level of comfort, ensuring that every visitor can find an option that aligns with their budget and expectations. Despite the differences in price and style, all park accommodations adhere to a high standard of service and are designed to elevate the overall Yellowstone experience by offering convenience, safety, and easy access to the park's natural attractions.

Venturing slightly outside park boundaries, visitors can also explore a wealth of nearby hotels and lodges that boast comfortable amenities and a warm welcome. These establishments, often located in gateway communities such as West Yellowstone or Gardiner, provide a convenient base for day trips into the park. Their intimate knowledge of Yellowstone's logistics and activities makes them valuable resources for planning your adventures, with many offering guided tours, local expert advice, and shuttle services that help bridge the gap between familiarity and the wild unknown of Yellowstone's interior.

## Reservation Systems and Strategic Planning

Given the enduring popularity of Yellowstone National Park, whether for camping spots or lodge stays, savvy travelers understand that early reservations are key to securing the perfect spot. During peak seasons, especially in summer months when the weather is most inviting, accommodations tend to book up months in advance. This is true for both camping sites and park lodges alike.

Most campgrounds and lodges in Yellowstone utilize online reservation systems that streamline the booking process. It is advisable to check the official Yellowstone National Park website, which continually updates availability, site descriptions, and any special conditions that might affect reservations. Additionally, some private lodging establishments maintain their own booking platforms, often featuring detailed descriptions of amenities, seasonal packages, and cancellation policies.

Taking time to read reviews and comparing prices can greatly assist in planning a seamless visit.

For RV travelers in particular, it is important to note that some campgrounds enforce strict rules on vehicle size and occupancy limits, making early research indispensable. Many visitors use online forums and social media groups dedicated to Yellowstone camping to share real-time updates about availability, weather conditions, and unexpected changes in campground management protocols. These community-driven insights can prove invaluable when trying to secure a reservation that meets your specific needs.

Considering peak periods such as national holiday weekends, summer breaks, and the shoulder seasons, it is wise to have a flexible itinerary and possibly even consider alternative travel dates. Such flexibility not only increases your chances of snagging an ideal campsite or lodge but also allows you the freedom to explore less-visited areas of the park. In the event that your preferred option is fully booked, having a backup plan—like reserving a site in a nearby community or even opting for a nearby privately owned campground—can ensure that your Yellowstone experience remains uninterrupted and enjoyable.

## Packing Essentials and Seasonal Gear: Preparing for Every Adventure

A successful stay in Yellowstone's campgrounds or lodges begins with thorough preparation. Packing is a crucial part of the planning process, given the unpredictable nature of the park's weather and the varying conditions across different seasons.

When camping, visitors should equip themselves with a comprehensive gear checklist. Essential items include sturdy tents with appropriate stakes and guylines, sleeping bags rated for the potential nighttime lows, and insulated sleeping pads for comfort on rugged terrain. Layered clothing is imperative—fast-drying, moisture-wicking fabrics are ideal for daytime hikes, while warm, waterproof layers are necessary for cooling evenings or unexpected rain. In areas close to geysers and hot springs, moisture-resistant gear can protect against sensitive steam bursts and condensation.

Cooking equipment is another critical element of your packing list. Many campgrounds provide picnic tables and fire rings; however, having a portable grill, a gas stove, and weatherproof utensils ensures that you can prepare hearty meals on-site. A cooler packed with perishables, along with resealable storage containers, is invaluable to keep food safe, while bear-proof food storage bags are recommended given the park's active wildlife community. Being prepared not only enhances your comfort but also minimizes the risk of encounters with bears and other wild animals attracted to improperly stored food.

For RV travelers, packing extends beyond personal items to include additional equipment specific to mobile living. An ample supply of water, extra fuel for generators, and a basic toolkit for unexpected repairs are essentials. Extra bedding, outdoor chairs, and compact shade tents can transform an RV campsite into a family retreat where evenings are spent laughing around a fire pit under starlit skies. Moreover, having a comprehensive first-aid kit easily accessible within your RV is a prudent measure in this remote setting.

Seasonal gear should be selected with care. During the summer months, sun protection—such as wide-brimmed hats, high SPF sunscreen, and polarized sunglasses—helps guard against intense ultraviolet rays. In winter, the park's environment transforms dramatically, requiring insulated thermal wear, waterproof boots, and additional fuel sources to maintain camping comforts in the colder months. Some campgrounds may offer limited services during the winter season, so ensuring you have independent supplies and emergency equipment is particularly important.

Aside from the standard camping items, many visitors find that including recreational gear can enrich their experience. Binoculars for wildlife observation, cameras with wide-angle lenses to capture the sweeping landscapes, and portable chairs for relaxing on sun-dappled afternoons lead to a more engaging and personalized visit. Even if you decide to stay in a lodge, a small daypack filled with essentials for spontaneous hikes can enhance your experience by allowing you to swiftly transition from a comfortable room to the rugged trails that define Yellowstone.

## Family-Friendly Camping and Accommodation Tips

Yellowstone's diverse accommodations cater to families with children, ensuring that both parents and kids enjoy a rewarding, safe, and educational experience. Family- friendly campgrounds feature not only open spaces for children to play but also amenities such as clean restroom facilities, picnic areas with grilling spots, and sometimes even designated play zones. These features create an environment where safety and fun exist in tandem.

For families opting to camp, it is beneficial to choose sites that not only offer space for tents and recreational vehicles but also opportunities for educational activities. Many campgrounds are located near centers where naturalists and park rangers host interactive sessions, introducing young explorers to Yellowstone's fascinating wildlife and geothermal wonders. Parents will appreciate the organized programs that engage children in hands-on learning, providing a balanced mix of guidance and independent exploration.

When staying indoors or opting for lodge accommodations, seek out properties with suites or connected rooms to maintain proximity among family members. Several lodges offer kid-friendly dining options, special programs, and complimentary shuttle services that make navigating the vast park less daunting for families with young children. A predictable schedule that includes both structured activities and free time allows families to enjoy group activities—like guided hikes or nature scavenger hunts—without feeling rushed.

It is also important to plan meals, snacks, and rest breaks carefully. Families often thrive on a mix of on-the-go snacks that are easy to pack and hearty meals that can be prepared efficiently at a campsite or lodge dining facility. In many cases, communal dining areas encourage families to interact with other travelers, thereby creating a mini-community of shared adventures and traveling tips. This interaction can be especially enriching for children, who learn the value of cooperation and community while experiencing the wonders of nature firsthand.

For those with children, safety is paramount. Ensure that your chosen camping or lodging location has clear guidelines on wildlife safety and emergency protocols. Campgrounds in Yellowstone are designed to minimize risks, but supervision is key, particularly when near water bodies or geothermal features. Preparing children for the realities of park wildlife—such as the importance of keeping a safe distance from bison or bears—establishes a respectful understanding of the environment.

Simultaneously, the park's ranger programs and interactive educational displays provide additional layers of instruction on how to behave safely while still enjoying every adventure the park has to offer.

## Guidelines for Responsible and Safe Camping

While enjoying the natural amenities of Yellowstone's campgrounds and lodges, practicing responsible camping ensures both your safety and the preservation of the park's unique environment. Yellowstone's enchanting vistas come with both beauty and responsibility, and maintaining sustainable practices is central to experiencing the park at its best.

Adhering to **Leave No Trace** principles is essential when camping in Yellowstone. This means that every visitor should pack out all trash, minimize campfire impacts by using designated fire rings, and ensure that all remnants of your activities are thoroughly cleaned up before departure. Many campgrounds provide waste disposal areas and recycling facilities, and using these designated spaces ensures that the environmental footprint of your visit remains minimal.

Understanding and following park rules is another pivotal component of a safe camping experience. Yellowstone is home to wild animals that roam the park's vast expanse freely; thus, policies such as storing food in bear-proof containers, never feeding wildlife, and keeping a safe distance from animals are strictly enforced.

Regular briefings by park rangers, posted guidelines in campgrounds, and educational programs help reaffirm these rules to every visitor. Ignoring these precautions not only puts you at risk but also disturbs the delicate balance of this natural wonder.

Nighttime in Yellowstone offers breathtaking stargazing opportunities, but it also requires careful planning. Campers should always have reliable lighting, such as headlamps or flashlights with extra batteries, to safely navigate around their campsite after dark. Keeping emergency numbers readily available and ensuring that someone in your group is familiar with first aid enhances your overall safety, especially in remote areas.

Fire safety, particularly important in a park renowned for its pristine forests, is another critical guideline. Always burn only in allowed areas, and ensure that fires are completely extinguished before leaving your campsite. Many campgrounds have fire bans in place during periods of high risk, so staying informed through park alerts and local news is essential. Equally, if you are using a stove or portable grill, ensure that these devices are placed at a safe distance from any flammable materials and that they are operated strictly according to the manufacturer's directives.

Adopting a respectful attitude towards the environment means that every camper shares the responsibility of safeguarding Yellowstone. Before setting up your tent or parking your RV, choose a site that does not disrupt surrounding vegetation or wildlife habitats. Following marked trails to campsite areas and refraining from creating new paths are practices that help preserve the integrity of the natural landscape for future visitors.

## Seasonal Considerations for Camping and Accommodations

Yellowstone National Park is a seasonal marvel where each time of year offers its own distinct experience. Understanding the seasonal shifts is key to selecting the right camping or lodging option and packing appropriate gear.

During the summer months, the park is abuzz with vibrant energy, attracting thousands of visitors eager to embrace long, sunlit days. Campgrounds may be bustling during this season, so arriving early or reserving spots well in advance is advisable. The warm, sunny weather allows for extended outdoor activities and nighttime campfires under the stars, but it also means planning for increased wildlife activity, particularly near food storage areas. In summer, high SPF sunscreen, insect repellent, and plenty of water are essential gear for those spending long days exploring the trails.

As the leaves begin to change in the fall, Yellowstone transforms into a canvas of reds, oranges, and yellows. With cooler temperatures and fewer visitors, fall can be a wonderful time for those seeking a quieter experience. Accommodations during this time, encompassing both campsites and lodges, are typically less crowded, offering an intimate communion with the park's stunning vistas. However, unpredictable weather changes demand that visitors pack warm clothing, layered gear, and rain protection for sudden showers or early winter chills. The crisp autumn air, combined with quiet, reflective days, creates a distinctive ambiance that many travelers cherish for its serenity and beauty.

Winter in Yellowstone is a season of hushed landscapes, where snow blankets the park and transforms it into a winter wonderland. While many campgrounds close their gates during the depths of winter, the park offers alternative lodging options such as winter lodges and designated winter camping areas for those who are well-prepared for extreme conditions. Winter travelers must equip themselves with specialized clothing, such as insulated jackets, waterproof boots, and thermal undergarments, in addition to carrying survival essentials like extra fuel and emergency supplies. The challenges of winter camping demand a higher level of preparation, but the reward of witnessing geysers steaming against a snowy backdrop is an experience that few ever forget.

Spring in Yellowstone bursts forth with new life as flora awakens from the dormant winter months. Campgrounds gradually reopen, and lodge bookings become available as the once-muted landscape transforms into a vibrant mosaic of wildflowers and flowing streams. During this transitional period, visitors may encounter intermittent weather conditions—sunny mornings often give way to brisk afternoons. Packing should emphasize versatility: light layers for daytime warmth and additional, insulated clothing for the cooler nights. Spring's allure lies in its balance of optimism and the caution needed to navigate a park on the verge of its annual renewal.

## Insider Tips for Securing the Perfect Spot

With a variety of camping and accommodation options available, a few insider tips can help visitors enhance their Yellowstone experience. First, timing is everything. Booking reservations as soon as the official dates become available is crucial, especially if you have a preferred site in mind. Many popular campgrounds and lodges fill their allotted spots months in advance, so early planning provides the best chance of staying exactly where you want.

Second, always check cancellation policies and alternative dates when making your reservations. While it may be disappointing to encounter a fully booked site, flexible travel dates can significantly increase your chances of scoring a spot that meets your needs. Networking with fellow travelers through online forums or local travel clubs can also yield valuable information about recent cancellations or less-known accommodations that offer a similar experience without the long wait lists.

Third, consider the length of your stay and the diversity of experiences you wish to have. Splitting your time among different areas of the park, such as spending a few nights at a convenient campground near geothermal features and switching to a lodge with modern amenities in another region, can provide a balanced view of what Yellowstone has to offer. This pattern not only prevents boredom from a single routine but also ensures exposure to a broader variety of natural landscapes and park features.

## Practical Considerations and Preparations

The right camping or accommodation decisions enhance your visit by minimizing stress and maximizing your enjoyment of Yellowstone's splendor. Preparing not only involves booking your spot ahead of time but also reading up on park maps, local regulations, and environmental guidelines that pertain to the specific site you choose.

Before making a reservation, spend time reviewing the site descriptions, available amenities, and any unique features that differentiate one campground or lodge from another. For RV travelers, double-checking site dimensions, parking configurations, and restroom facilities can help avoid last-minute disappointments once you arrive on site. Many websites offer interactive maps that detail the layout of campgrounds, and using these tools can assist in selecting a site that is both convenient and suited to your needs.

Once you've secured your reservation, create a detailed checklist of all items you plan to pack. Group supplies into categories such as cooking equipment, clothing, personal gear, recreational items, and safety equipment. A well-organized checklist allows you to quickly verify that no critical item is left behind. It also helps to review recent trip reports or updates posted by previous visitors as these can highlight new changes in amenities or unforeseen issues such as temporary closures or weather warnings.

Establishing a clear plan for food storage is essential when camping in an area with active wildlife. This might include portable bear-proof containers, cooler boxes with secure, tight-fitting lids, or even designated storage lockers that some campgrounds provide. By taking the extra step to ensure that all food items and scented products are stored safely, you not only protect yourself from potential wildlife encounters but also contribute to the overall safety and cleanliness of the campsite.

Making use of technology can also simplify your trip preparations. Download park maps on your mobile device, set up weather alerts, and maintain a digital copy of your reservations and permits. Consider investing in a portable power bank to keep your devices charged while on the go, ensuring that you can access important travel information at all times. Such careful planning can transform your trip from a potentially stressful logistical challenge into an enjoyable, well-managed adventure that allows you to fully appreciate Yellowstone's natural wonders.

## Balancing Comfort and Authenticity

One of the hallmarks of camping and accommodations in Yellowstone is the delicate balance between modern comfort and the authentic, raw experience of nature. Whether you choose a minimalist campsite or a fully serviced lodge, the park's offerings are designed to remind visitors of the symbiotic relationship between humanity and the natural world.

For the more adventurous traveler, campgrounds that offer a basic yet secure environment encourage a deeper immersion into the natural surroundings. Sleeping under a starlit sky, waking to the distant roar of a geyser, and hearing the soft murmur of wildlife creates an unrivaled sense of connection with Yellowstone that few other travel experiences can match. This minimalist approach to camping fosters mindfulness and encourages visitors to engage with the environment in a meaningful way.

Conversely, for those who may prefer periodic comforts—perhaps after long days of hiking or wildlife watching—the park's lodges offer luxury through carefully curated services. Even here, the emphasis remains on blending into the magnificent landscape. Many lodges feature large windows that frame panoramic views of the park, ensuring that while you enjoy modern amenities such as hot showers, comfortable beds, and gourmet meals, you remain constantly aware of the expansive beauty just beyond your window. In these settings, every detail, from the decor to service style, is intentionally designed to reflect the spirit of Yellowstone.

The choice between a campsite and a lodge may also hinge on personal needs and travel goals. A family looking to bond during an outdoor adventure may prefer the flexibility and intimacy of a campground. In contrast, those who have spent long hours trekking rugged trails might opt for a lodge that provides a restorative retreat at the end of an active day. Both experiences, however, share a common thread: an invitation to reconnect with the natural world, to pause and savor Yellowstone's stunning vistas, and to appreciate the care with which the park manages its dual role as both a natural sanctuary and a cherished travel destination.

## The Role of Local Expertise and Park Resources

Yellowstone National Park abounds with knowledgeable staff and local experts who provide invaluable insights that enhance your stay at any campground or lodge. Visitors are encouraged to speak with park rangers, concessionaire representatives, and local hospitality professionals to learn about the best practices for camping, current weather conditions, and any recent updates to park policies.

At many campgrounds, park ranger stations are conveniently located nearby, offering quick access to updated trail maps, emergency information, and wildlife safety guidelines. Engaging with these professionals can yield recommendations for less-traveled sites, hidden waterfalls, or even temporary exhibits that highlight the park's dynamic natural processes. Their firsthand accounts, combined with detailed historical context, create a layered narrative that deepens your appreciation of each unique camping or lodging experience.

Similarly, lodge staff are often well-versed in the local culture and natural history of Yellowstone. During breakfast or dinner service, they might share anecdotes about the park's evolving ecosystem or provide tips on the best times to view particular wildlife. Some lodges even host special events, such as evening talks led by local naturalists or guided stargazing sessions that explain the night sky's constellations as they appear over Yellowstone. These interactions cultivate a sense of community and shared purpose that can transform a simple overnight stay into an engaging educational journey.

## Weather Preparedness and Its Impact on Accommodations

Weather in Yellowstone is as unpredictable as it is beautiful—a factor that travelers must always respect when planning their camping or lodging arrangements. The regions of the park can experience dramatic shifts in temperature, wind, and precipitation, sometimes within a single day. This variability calls for a level of preparedness that ensures you can maintain comfort and safety regardless of the conditions.

For campers, weather readiness means always having extra layers of clothing, a waterproof tarp or canopy, and a plan for swift shelter if conditions change rapidly. In higher-altitude campgrounds, where temperatures may drop dramatically at night even in summer, investing in high-quality insulated gear can make the difference between a comfortable night's sleep and a restless one. Similarly, for lodge guests, while modern accommodations typically have climate control, it remains beneficial to have personal weather-related gear for excursions outside—such as wind-resistant jackets and moisture-wicking fabrics that adapt to the diverse climate of Yellowstone.

Monitoring weather patterns through local apps, park visitor centers, or even short-range radios ensures that you are never caught unprepared. Many seasoned campers recommend that visitors always have a contingency plan—whether that means identifying the location of nearby shelters or understanding the quickest route back to your campsite or lodge in the event of a sudden storm. This proactive attitude not only protects your physical well-being but also enhances your ability to enjoy the park's natural cycles safely.

## Enhancing the Experience Through Thoughtful Details

A memorable visit to Yellowstone extends beyond the basic necessities of shelter and food; it encompasses the thoughtful details that enrich your overall experience. For many who camp in the park, small touches such as personal photos hung outside a tent, a well-loved book on a portable camping chair, or even a carefully curated playlist that echoes the sounds of nature can transform a simple campsite into a truly personalized retreat.

Many campers take the time to document their experiences through journaling, photography, or sketching the countless vistas of the park. Integrating these practices into your camping routine not only deepens your own enjoyment but also serves as a lasting record of your adventure. In the quiet moments before dawn, while the park transitions from night to day, a single quiet reflection at the campsite can evolve into a profound appreciation of Yellowstone's seamless blend of grandeur and intimacy.

When choosing where to stay, considering the ambiance of a site can be as important as its practical facilities. Certain campgrounds are renowned for their serene nighttime environments, far removed from the bright lights and distractions of modern life. These spots offer an untouched slice of wilderness where quiet and solitude become almost tangible—a stark, welcome contrast to the structured comforts found in lodges. The choice, ultimately, rests on your personal preferences and what you wish to bring home from your time in Yellowstone.

In private cabins or lodges, thoughtful interior design that taps into local motifs and materials can create an atmosphere that feels both rugged and refined. From hand-carved wooden accents to locally inspired art, these details invite you to linger a little longer, to savor both the hard-won comforts of civilization and the raw beauty that surrounds you.

## Maintaining a Connection with Nature and Community

A fundamental ethos at Yellowstone is the commitment to maintaining a deep connection with nature while being mindful of the impact that every visitor has on the environment. Whether you choose the intimacy of a tent or the structured comfort of a lodge, the experience is designed not only for physical accommodation but also for a rejuvenation of the spirit. This is achieved through the interweaving of community spirit and communal respect for the land.

Campgrounds in Yellowstone tend to foster environments where stories and experiences are shared openly. Even a brief conversation with a fellow camper about the best time to witness the flurry of bison herds or the quiet window of opportunity to see an elk can lead to new perspectives and a richer appreciation of the park.

Participating in organized activities, such as ranger-led walks or interpretive talks available at many lodges, emphasizes that your stay is as much about learning and interacting as it is about resting.

Similarly, the careful design and historical resonance of many park lodges underscore how human ingenuity, when married with reverence for nature, can create spaces that honor the past while offering modern amenities. Many guests take time to listen to the stories of the park as recounted by long-time residents or staff members, and through these narratives, you can see how a commitment to sustainability and respect for nature has shaped the park's evolution. Whether in a shared lounge area, during mealtime conversations, or around communal fire pits in campgrounds, the blend of personal connection with environmental mindfulness becomes a cherished part of the Yellowstone experience.

## Embracing the Journey Through Mindful Preparation

Choosing the right camping or accommodation option is just one element of the larger journey that is a Yellowstone adventure. Mindful preparation, careful selection of a site that resonates with your travel goals, and a willingness to embrace the unexpected are keys to a fulfilling stay. Each site, whether it be under the open sky at one of the well-loved campgrounds or within the historical walls of one of the park's renowned lodges, offers its own narrative, a unique chapter in the greater story of Yellowstone.

As you plan your days of exploration, consider mapping out a variety of experiences. Spend a night at a secluded campground near a bubbling hot spring, then treat yourself to the rustic luxury of a lodge that allows you to recover and plan for the next day's adventure. Balancing these elements creates an itinerary that is both dynamic and restorative. The lessons of preparedness and flexibility become a constant undercurrent, ensuring that every moment, whether simple or extraordinary, adds value to your overall journey.

Leveraging the local expertise available—through park resources, local guides, or fellow travelers—enhances that personal itinerary. The shared human experience in Yellowstone, threaded through stories exchanged over shared meals or around a communal fire pit, reminds every visitor that while the landscape may be vast and wild, the spirit of camaraderie and collective respect for nature unites all who step into this storied national park.

# Final Thoughts on a Responsive and Inspiring Stay

Every facet of camping and accommodations in Yellowstone National Park is designed to complement both the rugged, untamed beauty of the environment and the thoughtful conveniences required by today's travelers. Every campsite, RV area, lodge, and nearby hotel is curated to provide safety, comfort, and an intimate connection to the unfolding drama of nature. From meticulous preparation and responsible food storage to engaging with local experts and fellow adventurers, your time in Yellowstone becomes a tapestry of personal discovery infused with the timeless spirit of the park.

Pay attention to subtle details—like weather updates, seasonal gear changes, and special programs offered by rangers—which will not only make your stay safer but also enrich your understanding of Yellowstone's living ecosystem. Thoughtful planning ensures that whether you are behind the wheel of an RV, setting up a tent in a quiet, secluded area, or checking in at a historic lodge, your experience is as rewarding as it is responsible.

Every moment spent here offers the chance to reconnect with nature in its purest form, to learn the timeless rhythms of geysers, wildlife, and whispering winds, and to capture memories that will last a lifetime. Yellowstone's camping and accommodations are not just about where you sleep—they are about embracing an authentic adventure set against one of the most awe-inspiring backdrops in the world.

By carefully selecting your ideal lodging, packing the necessary supplies, and adhering to safety and environmental guidelines, you set the stage for a transformative journey that honors both modern needs and the enduring majesty of the natural world. As you open your eyes to the sprawling vistas from your tent's canvas or the elegant window view in your lodge, you become part of Yellowstone's ever-evolving story—a narrative woven from the shared experiences of countless travelers who have, over generations, discovered that here in America's first national park, every moment is an invitation to explore, to learn, and to be truly alive.

# MAPS & ITINERARIES

Yellowstone National Park is a vast and intricate wonderland where every turn reveals new surprises. This section is designed to guide you through the exploration of Yellowstone's sprawling landscape with detailed maps and carefully structured itineraries. Whether you have only a day to spare or plan to immerse yourself in a week-long adventure, well-crafted maps and tailored itineraries ensure that your journey is efficient, immersive, and unforgettable.

## Overview of Yellowstone's Mapping System

Yellowstone's vast terrain necessitates a reliable mapping system. The park boasts a diverse array of attractions—

from thermal features and scenic overlooks to extensive hiking trails and abundant wildlife habitats—making a quality map not just a convenience, but a necessity. Professional cartographers and park rangers have collaborated over the years to produce detailed maps that highlight major thoroughfares, lesser-known trails, and interpretive markers.

The park maps are divided into several key categories: road maps, trail maps, and thematic maps. The road maps detail primary routes including park entrances, scenic drives, and major attractions such as Old Faithful, the Grand Prismatic Spring, Mammoth Hot Springs, Yellowstone Lake, and Lamar Valley. The trail maps exhibit the intricate network of hiking and biking trails that wind through forests, along rivers, and past geyser basins. The thematic maps offer focused insights for birdwatchers, wildlife enthusiasts, and those interested in geological phenomena, offering additional interpretative detail and historical context.

When planning your visit, it is advisable to obtain an updated version of these maps either from the park visitor centers or through official online resources. Digital maps on smartphones, when paired with offline capabilities, can be invaluable for real-time navigation in remote parts of the park. Nonetheless, keep in mind that cellular reception is limited in many areas, so having a printed or downloaded backup is a wise precaution.

## Interactive Tools and Digital Resources

Modern technology offers a blend of traditional mapping with innovative digital tools. In recent years, interactive digital maps have become indispensable for visitors who want to explore Yellowstone intelligently. These tools not only pinpoint your current location using GPS but also overlay points of interest, specify trail difficulty levels, and offer estimated driving distances and times. Many of these digital maps allow for personalized itinerary planning, enabling you to mark favorite sites—be they the erupting geysers or the serene vistas of the Lamar Valley.

Several official and third-party apps provide comprehensive, layered maps that include real-time updates on road closures, weather conditions, and wildlife sightings. These digital resources are seasoned with photographic highlights and detailed descriptions to enrich your journey. For families and active travelers alike, these tools foster a sense of spontaneity balanced with a structured plan, ensuring you never miss a critical stop or a hidden gem.

## Essential Elements for a Customized Visit

The art of successful exploration is not just in following a map, but in tailoring your route to your interests and energy levels. Yellowstone accommodates everyone from first-time park visitors to seasoned naturalists. Its vast array of attractions calls for itineraries that suit a variety of needs. Customizing your itinerary involves taking into account factors such as the time of year, weather conditions, wildlife activity, and the specific interests of your party.

For instance, if you are particularly interested in the geothermal wonders of Yellowstone, your itinerary might revolve around the Upper Geyser Basin and adjacent thermal features. Alternatively, wildlife enthusiasts might prefer routes that focus on the Lamar and Hayden Valleys, which are renowned for prime wildlife spotting opportunities. Families, seniors, and hikers all have distinct needs—whether it is shorter, more accessible trails or longer, more adventurous routes—and these factors will dictate the map routes that are most appropriate for your journey.

## Detailed Park Map Overview

A comprehensive park map is your visual guide to Yellowstone's immense territory. The central map usually divides the park into quadrants, with clearly marked entrances, visitor centers, rest areas, and interpretive signs. In the center, you'll often find the hub of activity around the Upper Geyser Basin. From here, multiple directions extend outwards—each representing a unique blend of historical significance and natural beauty.

The map highlights main roads such as the Grand Loop Road, a pathway that effectively links major attractions. Breakpoints on the loop indicate junctions from which side roads lead to slightly more secluded or specialized sites. Critical navigation markers include waypoints for the Auditorium, Madison, and Canyon areas, each featuring distinct geological formations and habitats. Detailed legends on these maps provide precise information about distances, road conditions, and seasonal advisories, allowing you to plan your route according to your physical needs and available time.

An integrated elevation profile is also a key feature seen on many high-quality maps. Yellowstone's topography is not uniform—ranging from elevated highlands to valleys carved by ancient rivers. Elevation markers highlight steep ascents and gentle slopes, vital for determining the difficulty of a hike or the energy expenditure required on longer drives. For visitors planning multi-day hikes, these details are invaluable in helping manage expectations and ensure that every step is taken with care.

## How to Navigate Yellowstone Using Maps

Before setting out on your route, take a few moments to orient yourself with the park's mapping system. Begin by identifying where you are on the main map—locate the primary entrance you will be using and trace the main road that leads to visitor centers. Establish your base point from which you can explore further. If you plan to visit the geyser basins, make sure your starting point aligns with the network of trails connecting these areas.

Always carry a printed copy of the map, even if you are relying on a digital solution. In remote parts of the park, battery-operated devices and offline maps become essential lifelines. Mark potential rest stops, picnic areas, and emergency kiosks along your planned route. Even a quick glance at an elevation marker or distance measurement can inform decisions about whether to extend a walk, turn back, or find shelter.

Understanding the scale of the maps is an additional critical element. The distances between attractions in Yellowstone are often more expansive than they appear on paper. Recognize that a map measuring in miles might not accurately represent travel time when accounting for winding roads, wildlife crossings, and varying speed limits. Adjust your expectations and plan buffer times accordingly.

For those interested in precise tracking, consider using a compass or GPS watch. These tools allow you to verify your position against the cartographic details, preventing any inadvertent detours into restricted or dangerous areas. In areas with significant elevation changes, such as the steep canyons or mountainous trails, knowing your precise location can enhance safety and enrich the overall journey.

## Suggested Itineraries for Every Traveler

Yellowstone's vast natural canvas allows for a multitude of itineraries designed to address different interests and time frames. Whether you have just one day, a long weekend, or an entire week to immerse yourself in the park, these detailed itineraries combine efficient planning with ample time to absorb the beauty of the surroundings.

### 1-Day Itinerary

A single day in Yellowstone can be a whirlwind of wonder if planned with purpose. Begin your day early at the park's primary entrance to maximize daylight hours. A well-structured 1-day itinerary might start with a drive along the Upper Loop of the Grand Loop Road, focusing on time-efficient highlights.

Your journey might commence at a major visitor center where you can receive updated maps and insider information. Then, set out to catch a glimpse of Old Faithful in the early morning before the crowds thicken. Pause briefly at the geyser basin to explore its surrounding boardwalks, ensuring safe distances from the active thermal features.

After witnessing Old Faithful's periodic eruptions, follow the road to the Midway Geyser Basin where Grand Prismatic Spring awaits. The best photos are taken shortly after sunrise, as the vibrant colors of the spring are further accentuated by the low morning light. Next, drive to the Biscuit Basin area for a quick, scenic walk if time permits.

As the day advances, venture towards Yellowstone Lake. This lacustrine getaway is perfect for an impromptu picnic and a moment of calm before you head west towards the Lamar Valley. Known for its wildlife, the Lamar Valley is ideal for a short stop to spot bison, elk, or even the elusive wolf. Conclude the day with a drive back to your starting point or nearest lodging, ensuring that every minute is maximized on your brief expedition through the park.

### 3-Day Itinerary

With a slightly extended schedule, a 3-day itinerary allows you to delve deeper into Yellowstone's multifaceted offerings. On day one, focus on the geothermal wonders. This day might mirror the 1-day itinerary with an expanded timeframe, starting with a comprehensive tour of the Upper Geyser Basin that goes beyond Old Faithful to include lesser-known thermal marvels. Allocate extra time for the Grand Prismatic Spring and the Fountain Paint Pot area, where you can immerse yourself in short hikes that reveal geothermal vents and bubbling mud pots.

The second day of your itinerary can be dedicated to exploring the natural history and diverse ecosystems of Yellowstone. Start early by driving to the Mammoth Hot Springs area. Here, the terraces of travertine formations present a landscape that is both surreal and historically rich, as these features have been formed over millennia. After capturing the intricate patterns with your camera, drive the scenic roads towards the Tower-Roosevelt area, where scenic vistas and wildlife are abundant. Enjoy a leisurely hike along one of the park's more relaxed trails—this is a great opportunity for families as well as seniors who appreciate less strenuous exploration.

On the third day, take a more scenic and wildlife-focused route. The Lamar and Hayden Valleys come into prominence on this day, favored by many experts as the best wildlife watching spots in the park. Start with an early morning drive in Lamar Valley to observe predators and grazing animals as they roam their natural habitat. Bring along binoculars and a field guide for local species to enrich your viewing experience. Conclude your 3-day journey with a visit to Yellowstone Lake, perhaps taking a small boat tour or simply relaxing by the water's edge, allowing the serene beauty of the largest high-altitude lake in North America to wash over you as you reflect on your diverse Yellowstone exploration.

### 7-Day Itinerary

A week-long expedition provides the luxury of truly savoring every facet of Yellowstone, allowing a slower pace and the ability to explore off-the-beaten-path treasures. A well-crafted 7-day itinerary allows for in-depth exploration of the park's regions, with certain days dedicated to specific thematic experiences.

Begin your week with a comprehensive tour of the geothermal areas. Over two days, explore not only Old Faithful and the Upper Geyser Basin, but also lesser-known thermal features such as the West Thumb Geyser Basin, where the interplay between hot water and Yellowstone Lake creates captivating thermal vistas. This extended exploration allows you to understand the dynamics of the park's geothermal phenomena thoroughly.

Spend the next two days focusing on historical and cultural landmarks. Explore Mammoth Hot Springs extensively, taking time not only to admire the travertine terraces but also to visit the interpretive exhibits that detail the human history of the area. Nearby, the Norris Geyser Basin offers a deeper dive into the science behind Yellowstone's volcanic activity. These days can be interspersed with leisurely walks, photography sessions, and stops at ranger-led talks that provide further background on the park's evolution and significance.

Dedicate the remaining days of your week to wilderness adventures and wildlife encounters. A full day can be allocated to exploring the Lamar Valley, where early morning and late afternoon light transform the landscape into a living panorama of roaming bison, elk, and even golden eagles soaring overhead. For those inclined to venture deeper, consider longer hikes or horseback riding tours facilitated by the park's certified guides, offering an intimate connection with nature.

On one of the evenings, incorporate a stargazing experience in one of Yellowstone's designated dark-sky areas. Away from artificial light, the clarity of the night sky allows the stars—and occasionally, the faint glow of the Milky Way—to captivate all who gaze upward. With each day planned meticulously on the map, you can venture off the main roads to smaller roads that lead to secluded campsites and interpretative spots, experiencing a more personalized connection with Yellowstone's essence.

## Tailored Itineraries for Specific Interests and Demographics

Yellowstone's versatility is best highlighted by the fact that its extensive network of trails and roads can be adapted for various types of travelers. Whether your priority is minimal walking or high-adrenaline adventure, there is an itinerary that fits your needs.

### Itineraries for Families

For families, the key is to blend adventure with convenience and accessibility. Many trails in Yellowstone are marked with clear signage, are relatively flat, and include interpretive stops that provide engaging insights about the environment. A family- oriented itinerary might include visits to the Junior Ranger Program centers, interactive exhibits at visitor centers, and short walks that are educational as well as fun.

Begin your day with a breakfast near the Old Faithful area, where kids can learn about the geyser's rhythmic eruptions. Move on to engaging trails with clear boardwalks and short stops, such as the Midway Geyser Basin, where the vibrant colors of Grand Prismatic Spring enchant both young and old. Incorporate picnic stops in safe, scenic areas near the lake to allow children to run and explore while benefiting from the park's natural amenities. For seniors in the family, ensure that breaks are incorporated regularly, and opt for accessible routes with minimal elevation gain. Additionally, ranger-led tours designed specifically for family members will often blend storytelling with scientific information in a way that captures the imagination of all age groups.

### Itineraries for Seniors

When designing itineraries for seniors, the emphasis should be on comfort, accessibility, and leisurely engagement with nature. Map out routes that avoid steep grades and excessively long walks, instead favoring scenic drives punctuated by short, leisurely stops. Many of the park's lookout points are easily accessible by vehicle, providing grand views with minimal walking.

A senior-friendly itinerary might feature extended time in the Mammoth Hot Springs area, where the unique trails, mostly constructed with firm and even surfaces, allow for a relaxed pace while admiring the ever-changing natural sculptures. Another valuable stop is the Norris Geyser Basin, where boardwalk paths are built with safety in mind and distance markers are clearly posted. Additionally, selecting stops with comfortable seating arrangements, picnic areas, and indoor exhibits ensures that senior visitors can absorb the park's rich heritage without the strain of continuous walking.

### Itineraries for Active Travelers

For those with a taste for vigorous adventure, Yellowstone offers itineraries that weave together strenuous hikes, invigorating drives, and off-road explorations. Active travelers can tailor their journeys to include multi-mile hikes, challenging climbs, and even parts of the park that require a more rugged approach.

A recommended plan involves mapping out a circuit that begins with an early morning run or bike ride along designated trails near the park's entrances, followed by a challenging hike through the more isolated sections of the Grand Canyon of Yellowstone. These itineraries often incorporate side trails that diverge from the main roads, leading to viewpoints that reward the effort with breathtaking panoramas. Be sure to carry a detailed trail map alongside a compass or GPS device, as the less-traveled paths can sometimes lack the distinct landmarks of the main thoroughfares. With dynamic options for hydration points, rest stops, and clearly marked distances, active travelers can confidently push their limits while enjoying a rigorous exploration of Yellowstone's inherent splendor.

## Planning Multi-Day Adventures with Integrated Mapping

Mapping out a multi-day journey through Yellowstone involves not only charting routes but also understanding the park's time-sensitive dynamics. The itineraries presented in this guide can be adapted based on seasonal conditions, park alerts, and personal energy levels. Dividing your days into thematic blocks allows for both intentional exploration and spontaneous discovery.

When planning a multi-day itinerary, allocate your days to cover different sections of the park. For instance, dedicate the early days to major attractions such as the famed geyser basins and geothermal areas. Using the park map, note the distances between these high-interest spots and incorporate buffer periods for unexpected wildlife activity or unscheduled stops. For each day's route, annotate critical stops on your map—a quick glance at highlighted points can remind you of photo opportunities, historical markers, and recommended safe spots to rest.

Incorporate a mix of short and long hikes to maintain a comfortable pace. For example, one day might consist of a brief, educational walk along a thermal trail, followed by a longer drive through verdant valleys conducive to wildlife spotting. Utilize color-coded overlays on your maps to differentiate between regions: one color for geothermal attractions, another for wildlife zones, and a third for scenic overlooks. Such visual indicators facilitate easier navigation and ensure that even the more extensive itineraries remain organized and accessible.

For visitors planning to camp within the park, detailed maps often include essential information on campground locations, available facilities, and designated RV sites. Each site is marked with potential hazards, fire safety instructions, and even restrooms. Note that some campgrounds fill up quickly, so use your itinerary maps to plan early visits on less popular days of the week or during off-peak hours when possible. Detailed directions provided by park rangers and printed maps help reduce last-minute navigation challenges, ensuring that transferring from one site to another is as smooth as possible.

When integrating mapping into your itinerary, consider building in periodic stops that allow for both rest and local exploration. Specific junctions on the map, such as the cross-roads near Yellowstone Lake or the trailheads adjacent to major thermal features, offer ideal settings for unpacking, refueling, and reviewing the next segment of your journey. Balancing extended exploration with deliberate rest stops creates an itinerary that is both ambitious and consistently rejuvenating.

## Utilizing Detailed Trail Maps for Scenic Driving and Hiking

Trail maps in Yellowstone are designed with layers of information that cater to hikers, bikers, and even horseback riders. These maps provide granular details such as trail difficulty ratings, estimated hiking times, water sources, emergency evacuation routes, and points where mobile coverage might be available. Color-coded markers indicate circuits suitable for novice hikers versus those that challenge experienced trekkers. Interpretive signage details along trails enrich your understanding of Yellowstone's ecological context, from geological formations to seasonal flora and fauna.

For the avid hiker, trail maps serve as more than just directional tools—they are gateways to a deeper understanding of Yellowstone's layered environment. Detailed annotations along trailheads enhance your expedition by providing historical context to rock formations, answers to natural mysteries like the formation of geyser basins, and insights into the behaviors of local wildlife. As you study these maps before setting out, take note of any alternate routes that might become appealing if primary paths are crowded or closed due to weather-related issues.

Drivers can benefit from similar detailed maps that emphasize scenic routes interwoven between major attractions. These maps include mileage markers, rest stops, and suggestions for impromptu photo sessions. Many scenic driving maps highlight the best viewpoints from which to enjoy the panoramic landscapes of Yellowstone. These stops can be critical for active travelers who want to balance long drives with the possibility of short hikes or photographic breaks in particularly picturesque locales.

For those exploring by bicycle or on foot, having an integrated mapping system that lays out alternative loops away from busy roads is especially beneficial. Bike trails are marked with directional arrows, distance indicators, and sometimes hazard warnings. This extra layer of detail ensures that even if you choose to break away from the main roads for a more intimate encounter with nature, your route remains clearly defined and mapped for safe passage.

## Incorporating Local Insights into Itineraries

Personalizing your itinerary can be enhanced by incorporating insights garnered from local experts, park rangers, and frequent visitors who understand Yellowstone's changing rhythms. Many detailed maps now include QR codes or references to online databases where you can check real-time updates on trail closures, geyser activity, and wildlife movements. These dynamic features bridge the gap between static maps and the living, breathing ecosystem that Yellowstone represents.

Local insights suggest varying itineraries based on seasonal variations. During spring and early summer, wildlife is particularly active in the lower valleys, prompting itineraries that maximize early morning drives through Lamar Valley or Hayden Valley. In contrast, autumn itineraries might focus on the dramatic change in foliage, with routes that include longer drives through forested areas where the changing colors provide a breathtaking backdrop. Similarly, winter itineraries—though requiring specialized gear and experience—can be mapped to include guided snowmobile tours or cross-country skiing paths, ensuring that even in the coldest months, the park's magic is accessible.

Many park rangers recommend that visitors allocate time to simply study the maps provided at each visitor center. These maps often carry hidden gems—small interpretive panels, unique geological outcrops, or quiet trails that are not widely publicized. By spending a few minutes with a park ranger, you can retrieve updated recommendations and even minor adjustments tailored to your interests. These momentary interactions might reveal that the best place to witness a rare wildlife sighting is a backroad that isn't always highlighted on standard maps. Integrating this localized wisdom with your planned itinerary makes your journey both informed and intimate.

## Creating a Versatile Itinerary for Every Interest

Yellowstone's itineraries are never one-size-fits-all. The beauty of the park lies in its multiplicity—each trail, road, and boardwalk telling a different story. For visitors with particular interests, whether it be geological exploration, wildlife observation, or cultural history, the itineraries are designed to adapt.

For the geology enthusiast, organize your itinerary to follow a circle of thermal areas that explain the park's volatile volcanic history. Start at Old Faithful and move clockwise along the Grand Loop Road, with stops at the Midway Geyser Basin, Norris Geyser Basin, and West Thumb Geyser Basin in a seamless circuit. Along the way, each map includes annotations that detail the chemical composition of the springs, the physics behind geyser eruptions, and historical accounts of early scientific discoveries in Yellowstone.

Wildlife enthusiasts benefit from itineraries that highlight the park's vast grasslands and forested areas. Craft a route that begins at sunrise in Lamar Valley, where the quiet of early morning increases the chances for calm, undisturbed animal observation. Follow up by making stops at roosting sites along the riverbanks or secluded forest clearing points, where local maps indicate optimal viewing spots. Many maps now mark "wildlife observation points" with unique icons, ensuring that you venture safely off the beaten track while remaining within the boundaries of protected zones.

For those with an appetite for cultural history, integrate short visits to visitor centers that house interpretive exhibits. These centers often provide additional layers of information, including historical photos, indigenous narratives, and the evolution of park management. Your itinerary might weave between these indoor educational stops and outdoor scenic drives, each highlighted on your map by room for exploration and introspection. Over the course of several days, these diverse interests are harnessed into a single, comprehensive route that is both educational and exhilarating.

## Tips for Customizing Your Itinerary

Flexibility is a cornerstone of a successful Yellowstone adventure. While printed and digital maps provide a structured framework, your itinerary should allow for spontaneity. Before setting out, mark all key locations of interest on your map, but leave room for unscheduled stops. Yellowstone is a dynamic environment where weather conditions and unexpected phenomena may necessitate quick changes to your planned route.

A few tips for itinerary customization include:

- **Check the Weather:** Utilize online resources and mobile apps that offer real-time weather updates. Adjust your itinerary based on sudden changes, and always have a backup plan.

- **Consult Ranger Stations:** Ranger stations are treasure troves of local knowledge. Whether it's tips on the current activity of geysers or the best spot for wildlife encounters on that day, slight modifications to your itinerary based on ranger recommendations can turn a good day into a great one.
- **Plan for Breaks:** Not every stop needs to be a major attraction. Use the maps to identify scenic pullouts, picnic areas, or designated rest zones where you can take a break, hydrate, and recalibrate your route.
- **Group Itineraries by Interest:** If traveling in a group with mixed interests, consider splitting the day into segments where part of the group explores one area while others delve into different attractions. Later, these paths may converge at a central meeting spot, marked on your maps.

Over time, as you gain familiarity with Yellowstone's mapping system, you may begin to blend structure with spontaneity more fluidly. Consider this process part of the adventure itself—a continuous dialogue between your planned itinerary and the living, breathing pulse of the park.

## Maps and Itineraries: Integrating Practical Safety and Enjoyment

While exploring Yellowstone's vast territory is a profound experience, it is essential to balance excitement with caution. Integrated within the mapped itineraries are safety guidelines that many park maps include. These guidelines offer critical reminders about unpredictable geothermal activity, wildlife behavior, and potential hazards along rugged roads or trails.

Pay special attention to caution symbols and notes on your maps. Areas surrounding thermal features are often marked with alerts advising visitors to maintain a safe distance from the edges and boardwalks. Similarly, wildlife observation points are set within designated viewing distances to protect both the animals and the visitors.

Many maps incorporate "Safety Zones" in which emergency call boxes or marked meeting points are available in case of sudden changes in weather or other emergencies. For multi-day itineraries, mark the locations of first-aid stations, ranger outposts, and exit routes. Integrate these into your daily schedule to afford reassurance and a clear plan for unforeseen circumstances. An awareness of your surroundings, as depicted through precise mapping, elevates both the enjoyment and the safety of your expedition.

## Finalizing Your Yellowstone Adventure Plans

Your map and itinerary are not static documents but living guides that evolve as you gain insight into the park's rhythms. Begin each day by reviewing your map, rechecking critical points such as trail entry points, scenic viewpoints, and necessary safety stops. Adjust your itinerary based on real-time observations and insights from fellow travelers or park staff.

An effective approach to managing your itinerary is to break down your days into morning, afternoon, and evening segments—each dedicated to a particular region or theme. For example, a morning segment might focus on exploring the geothermal wonders in short, accessible bursts, while afternoons are reserved for wildlife observation or gentle hikes. Evenings can be used for reflection and outdoor activities like stargazing or simply enjoying the solitude of a lakeside setting.

By aligning your activities with the tangible markers on your map, you create a rhythm that makes every moment of your visit purposeful and deeply engaging. Each mark and line on your map represents not only a path to discovery but also a chapter in your own unique Yellowstone adventure.

When planning your itinerary, consider the variables that influence travel within the park. Arrival times, seasonal road conditions, park events, and even recreational programs such as ranger-led tours can all dictate minor shifts in your plan. A printed itinerary, enhanced with annotations from local guides, serves as a robust framework that is resilient enough to accommodate such changes while preserving the overall structure of your journey.

Your journey through Yellowstone is as much about digesting the majesty of the natural world as it is about the thoughtful planning that leads you there. The maps provided, both in print and digitally, are more than simple directions—they are your gateway to discovery in one of America's most storied landscapes. Every clearly marked road, every highlighted trail, and every safety annotation on these maps converge to form a resource that is both inspirational and practical.

By harnessing the power of detailed mapping and personalized itineraries, your adventure in Yellowstone will be a blend of scientific inquiry, emotional engagement, and physical exploration. The interplay between well-delineated routes and your individual interests creates an itinerary that is uniquely yours, ensuring that every moment is as enriching and safe as it is awe-inspiring.

# SAFETY TIPS & PARK RULES

## Understanding Yellowstone's Uniquely Dynamic Environment

Yellowstone National Park is a landscape where nature's raw power is visible in every geyser eruption, boiling hot spring, and wandering herd of bison. From the moment you step into the park, you are entering an environment that demands respect and careful observation. The park's unique terrain, combined with its vibrant ecosystems, requires visitors to be well-informed about safety protocols and park rules. These guidelines are designed not only to protect you but also to preserve the natural beauty and dynamic ecosystems that have made Yellowstone an iconic destination for generations of explorers.

Yellowstone's environment is as diverse as it is breathtaking. Here, volcanic activity still shapes the ground you walk upon. The intricate network of geysers, hot springs, mud pots, and fumaroles creates microhabitats that are both scientifically fascinating and potentially hazardous if approached without caution. In addition to the geological phenomena, the park is home to a wide variety of wildlife, each species adapted to a unique niche within this vibrant ecosystem. Consequently, visitors are encouraged to adopt safety practices that respect both the inherent grandeur and the delicate balance of nature in Yellowstone.

## Wildlife Safety: Respecting the Park's Iconic Inhabitants

One of the most memorable aspects of Yellowstone is its abundant and diverse wildlife. However, the same animals that inspire wonder and awe can become dangerous if safety guidelines aren't followed rigorously. **Close encounters with wildlife can be unpredictable**, and the park has established clear protocols to prevent accidental and potentially harmful interactions.

### Maintaining a Safe Distance

It is crucial to maintain a safe distance from all wild animals. Wildlife in Yellowstone includes large mammals such as bison, elk, bears, and wolves. Bison, in particular, are responsible for more injuries in the park than any other animal. When observing bison, remain at least 25 yards away. For bears, a minimum distance of 100 yards is strongly recommended, especially during times of increased foraging activity. Use binoculars or a telephoto lens to get a closer view without disturbing the animals.

### Observing Animal Behavior

Understanding animal behavior can also improve your safety. If you notice an animal displaying unusual behavior—such as charging, bluffing with their posture, or making direct eye contact—it is vital to move away calmly and slowly. Never attempt to feed any animal, as close interactions can lead to habituation, diminishing their natural fear of humans and increasing the risk of aggressive encounters.

### Staying in Designated Viewing Areas

The park provides numerous designated viewing areas that are strategically located for safe wildlife observation. These areas are chosen based on ecological data and ensure that visitors can enjoy sightings with minimal disturbance to the animals. When using these areas, avoid climbing over barriers or stepping off trails; doing so disrupts not only the animals but may place you at risk. Often, additional signage will display reminders of proper distances and necessary precautions.

### Group Safety Practices

Traveling in groups can help reduce risk during wildlife encounters. When more people are present, there is a higher likelihood of spotting warning signs of animal agitation early. Groups can coordinate their movements, maintaining a quiet and controlled presence. Designate a leader who can direct the group's observations, ensuring that everyone is aware of where safety margins lie. An effective strategy is to appoint a "wildlife watcher"—someone who continually monitors animal behavior and alerts the group to any changes that might indicate potential danger.

### Specific Guidelines for Bear Country

Bears are often drawn to areas with abundant food sources, including improperly stored food or garbage left in camping areas. If you are planning to camp or picnic, keep all food in bear-proof containers provided by the park, or in your vehicle, especially if you are in backcountry areas. When hiking in bear country, consider carrying bear spray that is easily accessible. Learn how to use the spray properly by participating in ranger-led safety seminars offered within the park. If you unexpectedly encounter a bear, refrain from sudden movements and slowly back away while keeping your eyes on the animal. Never run; a bear's speed far exceeds that of a human, and running can trigger a chase response.

## Thermal Area Cautions: Appreciating Natural Wonders from a Safe Distance

Yellowstone's geothermal features are among the most extraordinary on the planet, but their mesmerizing beauty should not lure visitors into unsafe practices. The vividly colored hot springs and mud pots are the result of extreme geothermal activity, which makes them as dangerous as they are beautiful.

### Understanding the Risks

It might be tempting to lean over a safe barrier to get a closer look at the bubbling pools, but the mineral-rich water in these areas is typically at temperatures that can cause severe burns. The ground surrounding these features can be unstable and deceptively thin. Stepping away from designated viewing points could result in serious injury or death. **Thermal areas are not meant for exploration beyond established paths**; even when the air appears to defy gravity, the stability of underlying earth can be compromised without warning.

### Adhering to Marked Trails and Boardwalks

Yellowstone has constructed boardwalks and trails around thermal areas to ensure that visitors can enjoy these natural wonders safely. Do not try to circumvent these paths or use a mobile device to assess where it might be safe to step. Respect all signs and warnings posted near geothermal features. These paths have been designed after thorough scientific analysis and are the best way to appreciate the wonders safely. Remember that boardwalks and paths are there to protect you from the often invisible dangers lurking in the fragile ground beneath.

### Education and Awareness

Before venturing near any thermal area, invest time in reviewing informational displays provided by park rangers and interpretive centers. These displays offer detailed insights into the science behind geothermal features and underline the critical reasons for maintaining a safe distance. Being informed emphasizes that **geological beauty comes with inherent risks**, and only through vigilant observation and strict adherence to guidelines can one safely enjoy these wonders.

## Weather Awareness and Emergency Preparedness

Yellowstone is subject to rapidly changing weather conditions that can turn a pleasant day into a potentially dangerous situation in a matter of minutes. Visitors should be prepared for unexpected shifts in climate, from sudden rainstorms in the summer to snow and sub-zero temperatures outside of peak seasons.

### Monitoring Weather Forecasts

Before embarking on your Yellowstone adventure, check reputable weather sources for any alerts or drastic changes in weather predicted for your visit days. In remote areas of the park, cell service is limited, so having an updated downloaded weather report on a mobile device or a portable weather radio is invaluable. Pay attention to the park's electronic signage at visitor centers and trailheads, as these are updated with current weather advisories, especially during the summer months when thunderstorms are common.

### Layering and Cold-Weather Gear

Even in the warmer months, Yellowstone can experience sudden drops in temperature, particularly in the early morning or at higher elevations. Dressing in layers is highly recommended. A moisture-wicking base layer paired with an insulating mid-layer and a waterproof, windproof outer layer will help you adjust to changing conditions. Always include a hat and gloves in your travel kit, as these simple items can make a significant difference during unexpected weather shifts.

### Dealing with Lightning

Thunderstorms are a common occurrence in Yellowstone during the summer months. When lightning is a possibility, creating a safety plan is paramount. Avoid open spaces, hilltops, and the vicinity of tall objects; instead, seek shelter in a car or a substantial building. If you are caught outdoors without shelter, crouch low to the ground with your feet together and minimize contact with the ground until the storm passes. Familiarize yourself with designated lightning safety zones within the park and always heed the advice of park rangers during storm conditions.

### Emergency Supplies and First Aid

In an environment as vast and unpredictable as Yellowstone, carrying a well-stocked emergency kit is not optional—it is essential. Your kit should include a high-quality first aid manual, any personal medications, a flashlight with extra batteries, a multi- tool, and a whistle to signal for help. Ensure that you have a working map of the area and that at least one member of your group is familiar with the park's navigation routes. For those venturing into remote backcountry areas, a personal locator beacon (PLB) or satellite messenger can be a lifesaver. These devices can transmit your location to rescue services even when traditional cell signals are unavailable.

### Establishing a Communication Plan

Since Yellowstone's cellular coverage is inconsistent, it is wise to establish a communication plan before beginning any hike or road trip through the park. Inform someone outside the park of your itinerary and expected return time. At the start of each day's adventure, check in with fellow travelers or park personnel if possible.

Knowing the locations of ranger stations and emergency call boxes along popular routes ensures that you have multiple avenues for help if needed. This planning minimizes the risk of being stranded or injured without a means to alert emergency services.

## Road Safety and Navigating the Park's Highways

Driving through Yellowstone National Park offers visitors unparalleled views and direct access to remote wonders, but it also comes with unique challenges that require careful attention.

## Safe Driving Practices

When driving inside the park, it is important to remember that wildlife and other unexpected hazards can appear on the road at any time. Always drive at or below the posted speed limits, and be prepared to stop suddenly. The park's winding roads demand constant vigilance—stay awake, avoid distractions, and refrain from using your mobile device while driving. Maintain a safe distance from the vehicle ahead and be cautious in areas where animals are known to cross the roads, particularly during dawn and dusk.

## Adhering to Road Signs and Speed Limits

Yellowstone's road system is designed with both visitor access and wildlife preservation in mind. Road signs are strategically placed to warn drivers of upcoming curves, wildlife crossings, and potential hazards. Respect these signs and heed any temporary speed restrictions that may be in effect due to weather or increased pedestrian activity. These measures are in place not only to keep you safe but also to minimize your impact on the natural environment and the wildlife that call it home.

## Preparation for Remote Driving Conditions

Given the park's remote areas and variable road conditions, it is recommended that you carry an emergency roadside kit. This kit should include basic tools such as jumper cables, tire repair materials, and water. In winter months, when roads can be icy or covered with snow, having chains or snow tires installed on your vehicle is imperative. Regular vehicle maintenance—checking tire pressure, brakes, and fluid levels—cannot be overemphasized for ensuring your safety during long drives through rugged terrain.

## Parking and Stopping Regulations

When you need to take a break to enjoy the scenery or explore nearby trails, always use designated parking areas. Iconic viewpoints and trailheads have established parking lots that are strategically placed to protect both you and the park environment. Illegally parking or stopping in areas where vehicles impede traffic flow or block sightlines can lead not only to fines but also to dangerous situations for other visitors and wildlife. Adhering strictly to these protocols helps preserve the safety and beauty of Yellowstone's roadways.

# Emergency Contact and Communication Protocols

No matter how meticulous your planning, emergencies can occur. Yellowstone National Park is vast, and having a clear emergency communication strategy is essential for every visitor.

## Knowing Where to Turn in an Emergency

Familiarize yourself with the location of the nearest visitor centers and ranger stations along your planned route. These stations serve as information hubs and are designed to coordinate emergency responses. In critically remote areas, note the locations of emergency call boxes and ensure that your mobile device is charged as much as possible before venturing far from civilization. Knowing these key points of contact can save precious minutes in a crisis situation.

## Establishing a Plan of Action

Before exploring the park, establish a clear plan of action with your travel companions. Arrange designated meeting points in case your group becomes separated unexpectedly. Share your itinerary with a friend or family member who is not visiting Yellowstone so that someone is always aware of your location. Establishing this plan in advance creates a safety net that can be activated quickly when needed.

### Utilizing Park Resources

Park rangers undergo extensive training to handle a variety of emergency situations, from medical incidents to wildlife encounters and sudden weather changes. Do not hesitate to contact park services if you encounter an emergency situation. Rangers are equipped with the knowledge and tools necessary to provide first aid, locate missing individuals, and manage hazardous weather events. Take a few moments to review the park's official guidelines on emergency procedures provided at visitor centers, and observe any posters or literature about what to do if you are lost or injured.

### Communication Devices and Their Proper Use

In areas where cell service is unreliable, reliance on alternative communication devices becomes essential. Satellite phones, two-way radios, or personal locator beacons (PLBs) are valuable investments for those planning to explore the backcountry or remote areas of the park. Learn how to operate these devices prior to your trip, and always carry them in an easily accessible part of your backpack or vehicle. These equipment options provide a vital link to emergency services when traditional communication methods fail in vast natural landscapes.

## Leave No Trace Principles and Responsible Tourism

Preserving the integrity of Yellowstone National Park is in the hands of every visitor. Responsible tourism is about enjoying the park's treasures while minimizing your impact on the environment. By following **Leave No Trace** principles, you contribute not only to your personal safety but also to the long-term sustainability of this irreplaceable natural wonder.

### Minimizing Human Impact

Every step you take in Yellowstone has the potential to affect the delicate balance of its ecosystems. Learn and practice the seven core principles of Leave No Trace:

- **Plan ahead and prepare:** Make informed decisions that minimize waste and prevent unintentional damage to natural resources.
- **Travel and camp on durable surfaces:** Stick to established trails and campsites to protect fragile soils and vegetation.
- **Dispose of waste properly:** Pack out everything you bring in, and use provided waste disposal systems to keep the park pristine.
- **Leave what you find:** Refrain from picking plants, disturbing wildlife, or taking natural souvenirs that diminish the park's wild character.
- **Minimize campfire impacts:** Use established fire rings, and opt for alternative cooking methods when possible to reduce the risk of wildfires and soil damage.
- **Respect wildlife:** Observe animals from a safe distance, and never feed or attempt to interact with them.

- **Be considerate of other visitors:** Maintain a peaceful and respectful environment for everyone to enjoy the natural landscape.

## Educating Yourself and Others

Taking time to educate yourself about the park's ecosystems, native species, and conservation efforts is both rewarding and essential for responsible tourism. Engage with ranger-led programs and educational exhibits found at visitor centers. Learn not only the proper ways to observe and interact with the park but also how your actions can impact the broader ecological network. Sharing this information with fellow travelers fosters a community of care and mutual respect, ensuring that Yellowstone's splendor is preserved for future generations.

## Enforcing Rules Through Understanding

Understanding and internalizing the reasons behind each regulation integrates a sense of purpose into every action you take in Yellowstone. Park rules such as staying within designated areas, adhering to designated routes around sensitive ecosystems, and using approved facilities for camping are enforced to balance human enjoyment with ecological preservation. When visitors see these rules not as restrictions, but as necessary safeguards, the overall experience becomes more meaningful and sustainable.

# Guidelines for Camping and Outdoor Activities

Whether you are an experienced camper or a first-time visitor planning a scenic picnic, the structured guidelines for camping and outdoor activities in Yellowstone are designed to ensure your safety and maintain the park's natural integrity.

## Selecting a Campsite Wisely

Yellowstone offers a range of camping options—from well-maintained campgrounds with fresh water and restrooms to backcountry sites that provide an immersive wilderness experience. Before setting up camp, choose areas designated for camping. Campgrounds are often situated in regions that have been evaluated for environmental impact, ensuring that your stay does not disturb wildlife or natural flora. For those venturing into more isolated areas, always check in with park rangers to obtain the necessary permits and guidance on local regulations.

## Food Storage and Wildlife Protection

Food storage at campgrounds is a critical safety measure given the park's active wildlife. Ensure that all food is stored in bear-proof lockers provided at most established campgrounds. If these facilities are not available, store food in your vehicle, away from sleeping areas. Do not leave any food or scented items unattended, and always clean your cooking area thoroughly after meals. These practices protect you from potential wildlife encounters and preserve the natural behavior of animals by preventing them from getting accustomed to human food.

## Fire Safety and Cooking Practices

Campfires are a cherished part of the camping experience, yet in an environment as dry and volatile as Yellowstone, they must be handled with extreme caution. Always use designated fire rings, and never build a fire outside of these areas. Keep a supply of water or a fire extinguisher nearby to quickly manage any unexpected flare-ups. Observe local fire bans or restrictions that might be in place during periods of high risk.

When cooking, use approved stoves and griddles, and avoid portable fires in areas that have not been officially designated as safe for such activities. Keeping responsibility for fire safety as a top priority minimizes the risk of wildfires and protects both visitors and wildlife.

### Trail Etiquette and Group Behavior

Yellowstone's extensive network of trails offers incredible opportunities for exploration. When hiking, maintain a moderate group size to preserve the quiet and solitude of the trails for others. Keep noise to a minimum and avoid littering along the path. In areas known for wildlife crossings, keep your group together to avoid stray members wandering too close to dangerous animals. If you're traveling with children, ensure they understand the importance of staying on the trail and the reasons behind every safety precaution. Respect for the trail not only enhances your own experience but also demonstrates courtesy to fellow explorers and contributes to the preservation of nature.

## Complying with General Park Regulations

Yellowstone National Park has a robust set of regulations and guidelines designed to protect both visitors and the park's natural resources. Understanding and complying with these rules is essential to ensure a safe and enjoyable journey through this unique landscape.

### Admission and Permit Requirements

Every visitor must adhere to the park's admission and permit guidelines. National Park Passes are required for access to Yellowstone, and some areas within the park may require additional permits, particularly for backcountry camping or specialized activities such as commercial filming or scientific research. Familiarize yourself with the park's official website prior to your visit to obtain current information on fees and permit requirements. Have these documents readily available, as park rangers may conduct random checks to ensure compliance with park protocols. This adherence supports park maintenance and contributes directly to ongoing conservation efforts.

### Adherence to Designated Trails and Areas

Many of Yellowstone's remarkable sights are accessed via established trails and boardwalks. Straying from these designated routes not only puts you at risk but may also cause damage to fragile ecosystems that have taken centuries to develop. Respect all markers and signage, and be patient if certain trails are temporarily closed due to maintenance, wildlife activity, or weather conditions. The guidelines governing trail access are based on scientific studies and environmental impact assessments and are devised to protect vital habitats and geological formations.

### Prohibited Activities and Ethical Considerations

There are several activities that are strictly prohibited in Yellowstone for safety and conservation reasons. For instance, off-road vehicle use is generally not allowed except on designated roads. Similarly, collecting rocks, plants, or relics is forbidden; these actions disturb the natural balance and can lead to degradation of the park's cultural and ecological heritage. Recreational activities that risk introducing non-native species—such as fishing without proper licenses or plant transplantation—are also heavily regulated. Ensure that any activities planned during your visit are in full compliance with park regulations, and check with park authorities if you have any doubts.

Upholding these rules not only fosters a safe environment but also sustains the park for future visitors.

### Interacting with Local Officials

Yellowstone National Park is managed by highly experienced local officials and park rangers, whose primary duty is to protect both visitors and the park's natural resources. It is important to cooperate fully with them, follow their advice, and adhere to any instructions given during an emergency or routine patrols. Engaging respectfully with park officials is essential; they are not just enforcers of rules but also valuable sources of local knowledge and safety information that can enhance your overall experience.

## Safety Practices for Specialized Activities

Yellowstone offers a myriad of adventure opportunities that can be both thrilling and demanding. Whether you are engaged in hiking, backcountry camping, or photography excursions, specialized safety practices should be incorporated into your travel plans.

### Hiking in Varied Terrain

The park's trails vary greatly in difficulty and environmental exposure. Prior to embarking on any hike, assess the trail's difficulty level, elevation gain, and length. Choose trails that align with your fitness level and expertise. For more challenging hikes, ensure you have a detailed map, sufficient water, and the necessary navigational tools. It is also wise to inform someone at the starting point of your estimated route and expected return time. In strenuous or less-traveled areas, taking regular breaks and monitoring your energy levels is essential to avoid fatigue-related hazards.

### Photography and Observational Activities

Many travelers visit Yellowstone with photography in mind, capturing breathtaking vistas and close-up encounters with wildlife. However, while setting up your equipment and waiting for the perfect light, never lose sight of your surroundings. Camera equipment can sometimes distract from critical environmental cues, so maintain situational awareness and ensure that you are not inadvertently encroaching on restricted areas or getting too close to wildlife. When positioning your tripod or other gear in designated areas, ensure that you are not obstructing pathways or causing inadvertent harm to the natural setting. Always remain flexible with your photography session so you can promptly adjust if the situation around you changes suddenly.

### Water-Based Activities

Water bodies such as Yellowstone Lake offer unique recreational opportunities, including boating and fishing. However, water-based activities in the park require their own set of safety precautions. When engaging in boating, always wear a life jacket, adhere to speed limits on the water, and operate your vessel only in permitted areas. The local weather can influence water conditions rapidly—sudden winds and fog can reduce visibility, and currents near shorelines can be stronger than anticipated. If you plan to partake in fishing, make sure you have the appropriate permits and follow catch-and-release guidelines that help maintain the local fish population. Familiarize yourself with watercraft regulations posted in and around the lake to ensure a safe and enjoyable experience.

# Managing Interpersonal Health and Group Dynamics

Safety within Yellowstone is also about the people traveling as much as it is about nature itself. Managing group health, addressing common illnesses, and preparing for interpersonal emergencies are all part of responsible travel in an environment that can be both physically demanding and emotionally exhilarating.

## Staying Hydrated and Nourished

When exploring Yellowstone's diverse landscapes, dehydration and fatigue can quickly turn a fun excursion into a hazardous situation. Pack sufficient water and nutritious snacks for every outing. In remote areas where help might not be readily available, having a reliable water filtration device and energy-rich, non-perishable foods can be crucial for maintaining group health. Regular hydration breaks during hikes and long drives are essential to prevent heat exhaustion and maintain alertness on the trail.

## Recognizing and Responding to Altitude Sickness

Some areas of Yellowstone, especially those at higher elevations, can cause altitude sickness in visitors who are not acclimated to thinner air. Symptoms may include headaches, nausea, dizziness, and shortness of breath. If you or a member of your group begins to exhibit these signs, it is important to stop, rest, and hydrate. In severe cases, descending to a lower elevation can alleviate symptoms rapidly. Always have a plan for this scenario and know the location of the closest medical facilities or ranger stations where help is available.

## Communication and Conflict Resolution Within Groups

Traveling with family or friends, especially on multi-day excursions, requires a cooperative mindset. Establish open communication channels within your group before setting out, ensuring that every member is aware of the safety plans, meeting points, and emergency contacts. Assign responsibilities based on individual strengths — someone might be responsible for navigation while another manages first aid supplies. Should conflicts or safety concerns arise within the group, approach them calmly and with a spirit of compromise. A cohesive group dynamic is vital for maintaining safety during unexpected incidents, and simple, respectful communication can alleviate tension while ensuring that everyone remains focused on shared objectives.

## Health Precautions and First Aid

Bring a well-stocked first aid kit that is appropriate for the park's environment. The kit should include blister treatment, antiseptics, bandages, and any personal medications. Familiarize yourself with basic first aid procedures, and consider taking a certified first aid course before your trip. Certain areas of Yellowstone are remote, and knowing how to treat minor injuries or common ailments can prevent complications. Should any health emergencies arise, contact park services immediately and be prepared to provide detailed information about your location and condition.

# Interaction with the Natural World Through a Lens of Safety

Every moment spent in Yellowstone is an opportunity to connect with nature's most unguarded and powerful forces. By integrating safety precautions into every facet of your visit, you not only protect yourself but also contribute to the conservation efforts that make this park a treasure for all. From the breath-taking geysers to the roaming herds of animals that have lived here for centuries, Yellowstone demands a respect that is reflected in the way you plan, behave, and interact with the environment.

While each individual safety measure plays its own role, it is their combination— understanding wildlife behavior, adhering to thermal area guidelines, preparing for variable weather, ensuring safe driving practices, and being ready for emergencies— that forms the backbone of a safe and responsible visit. Yellowstone's park rules are not arbitrary restrictions; they are the legacy of decades of research, conservation, and experience, iteratively refined to ensure that every visitor can marvel at nature's splendor without compromising safety or ecological integrity.

Maintaining a balanced perspective allows you to navigate the park with confidence. Each guideline, from wearing layers for fluctuating temperatures to carefully selecting a lineage-approved campsite, reinforces an awareness that heightens your appreciation for every turn of Yellowstone's rugged trails. Whether capturing the fleeting brilliance of a geyser or quietly observing a herd of bison grazing in the distance, your proactive approach to safety ensures that each spectacular moment remains a cherished, secure memory.

For many, Yellowstone becomes not only a travel destination but a lifelong standard for respect towards nature. By observing these safety tips and park rules, you embrace a philosophy that prioritizes learning, preservation, and responsibility. This engagement with the environment encourages ongoing dialogue between visitors and park management, ensuring that Yellowstone's fragile ecosystems are maintained even as they continue to inspire and educate future generations.

The permanent installations of safe boardwalks around steaming thermal areas, the uniformly posted wildlife observation signs, and the widely accessible emergency communication devices all form a tapestry of security woven into the very fabric of Yellowstone. This tapestry is supported by the commitment of every visitor who chooses to travel with mindfulness and respect. Making informed decisions about where to set up camp, how to share trails with wildlife, and when to seek shelter during adverse weather conditions all contribute to a safer, more enjoyable experience that aligns with Yellowstone's core values of conservation, education, and community.

Refining your itinerary with these safety pointers in mind will ensure that your journey through Yellowstone is not only aesthetically enriching but also methodically secure. When exploring geological marvels, following designated paths, or engaging in outdoor activities, each moment is an invitation to internalize the discipline that nature demands. Guided by well-established protocols and the collective wisdom of park experts, your adventure in Yellowstone becomes a harmonious blend of excitement and caution—a narrative that underscores the essence of responsible tourism.

Every decision, from choosing the appropriate hiking footwear to using a personal locator beacon in remote areas, builds towards making your journey as safe as it is memorable. The safety practices you integrate at each step strengthen not only your individual experience but also help safeguard the park's enduring legacy. Yellowstone's unique blend of fire and water, of erupting geysers and quiet meadows, demands that each visitor contributes to its continued preservation through thoughtful, informed, and careful action.

By embracing this comprehensive approach to safety, your visit transforms into an educational expedition where every guideline serves as a reminder of nature's power. The rules set forth by Yellowstone empower visitors to enjoy its splendor responsibly and ensure that all who follow these practices leave with a deeper understanding of the natural world and a profound respect for its preservation.

# FUN & EDUCATIONAL ACTIVITIES

Yellowstone National Park is not only a visual feast of natural marvels but also a living classroom where every trail and geyser offers an opportunity to learn. The park's commitment to fostering environmental awareness, scientific curiosity, and family bonding comes through a plethora of engaging activities. Here, native conservation efforts, interactive programs, and immersive outdoor experiences converge to create a rich tapestry of fun and educational opportunities for visitors of all ages.

## Junior Ranger Program: Igniting Curiosity and Stewardship

One of the park's crown jewels in educational outreach is the **Junior Ranger Program**. Designed specifically for young visitors, this program empowers children to discover the wonders of Yellowstone through a series of hands-on and interactive challenges.

When you arrive at the park's visitor center, you'll often find the Junior Ranger booklets stocked with questions, puzzles, and activities tailored to provide an informative yet entertaining exploration of Yellowstone's unique ecosystems. The program encourages children to engage with the environment actively. By exploring designated trails, observing geysers, and learning about geothermal features, kids gain an in-depth perspective on the park's natural history.

Families find it rewarding to work together—completing quizzes, participating in scavenger hunts, and even undertaking role-playing scenarios that mimic the work of park scientists and conservationists. Each completed activity earns them a stamp, and at the end of their journey, children are presented with a Junior Ranger badge and certificate. This tangible reward not only instills a sense of achievement but also encourages youngsters to become ambassadors for nature, fostering a lifelong passion for the outdoors and responsible conservation practices.

A typical Junior Ranger session might begin at a ranger-led introduction where experienced educators share fascinating stories about Yellowstone's geological background, the creation of its diverse habitats, and the importance of protecting endangered species. These interactive talks are infused with real-life examples, such as the cycles of the geysers and the behavior of the park's wolf packs, making abstract scientific concepts accessible to young minds. As children traverse marked trails, they encounter interpretive signs that detail the natural processes at work. The language is simple yet engaging, often featuring fun illustrations and challenges to maintain their attention and spark conversations among family members.

The program is not confined to a single location or time of year. Seasonal adjustments allow the Junior Ranger activities to highlight different park phenomena—from the blooming wildflowers in spring and the lively wildlife interactions in summer to the crisp, reflective beauty of the fall season. Special themed days, often held during public holidays or school breaks, provide an extended curriculum that includes arts and crafts based on Yellowstone's natural features. In these sessions, children may create models of hydrothermal features or design posters that celebrate the park's natural legacy. The Junior Ranger Program, therefore, becomes a bridge between education and recreation, ensuring that learning occurs naturally as families enjoy the great outdoors.

## Capturing Yellowstone: Photography and Nature Journaling

For those with an eye for detail and a passion for creativity, Yellowstone offers unbeatable opportunities for photography and nature journaling. Some of the most iconic spots such as Old Faithful, the vivid hues of Grand Prismatic Spring, and the sprawling expanse of the Lamar Valley serve as perfect backdrops for nature photography tutorials and creative writing workshops organized within the park.

Photography enthusiasts can attend guided sessions led by experienced photographers who impart tips on capturing the perfect light at dawn or twilight, techniques for photographing moving water, and tricks to frame the vast landscapes effectively. These sessions are tailored for all levels of photography skills. Beginners learn the basics of composition and natural lighting, while more advanced hobbyists explore settings on their digital cameras to capture the subtle nuances of Yellowstone's changing scenery. Whether you're using a smartphone or a professional-grade camera, the guidance provided helps you document your adventure in a way that tells your unique story of the park.

Alongside photography, many park visitor centers host workshops on nature journaling. These sessions encourage visitors to sketch and note down the myriad details of their surroundings—the texture of a rocks formation, the sound of bubbling hot springs, the playful interactions among wildlife, and the ever-changing colors of the sky. Participants learn how to use their senses to observe nature more deeply and record their findings in creative ways. Journaling not only enriches your visit but also serves as a personal record of your exploration, capturing emotions, findings, and memorable moments that can be cherished for years to come. The combination of photography and journaling provides a creative outlet that brings the scientific and artistic facets of Yellowstone together.

## Stargazing: A Celestial Classroom Under the Big Sky

The vastness of Yellowstone extends from its terrestrial features right up into the night sky, making stargazing one of the park's most enchanting and educational experiences. With minimal light pollution, the park offers an almost unrivaled view of the cosmos. Visitor centers and ranger programs often include stargazing sessions where knowledgeable guides lead groups through constellations, share legends associated with star formations, and explain the marvels of the Milky Way.

During these guided stargazing events, participants gather at designated open fields equipped with astronomy kits and telescopes. Rangers provide insights into the ancient navigation techniques used by indigenous peoples and early settlers, illuminating how different cultures interpreted the stars. These sessions often begin with an introduction to astronomical basics: understanding the motion of celestial bodies, differentiating planets from stars, and learning about the significant astronomical events that occur throughout the year. As the night deepens, guides share fascinating narratives about meteor showers, eclipses, and even the science behind the northern lights, where conditions permit.

Even families with young children benefit from these nocturnal adventures. Interactive games are incorporated into the stargazing experience, such as "star story time" where groups collaboratively invent stories about the constellations, blending folklore with modern astrophysics. These moments not only kindle an interest in science and astronomy but also strengthen family bonds as you marvel together at the infinite beauty above. The stargazing experience in Yellowstone serves as a dynamic classroom where both the mysteries of the universe and the practical aspects of night- time safety and gear use are addressed, leaving everyone with a deeper respect for nature's grandeur.

## Picnic Areas and Natural Learning Zones

Yellowstone's thoughtful design includes numerous picnic areas that double as natural learning zones. Carefully chosen for their beautiful vistas and safe environments, these spots allow families to enjoy a meal together while being immersed in the park's natural splendor. Each picnic area comes with informational signs detailing local flora and fauna, fascinating facts about the geology of the region, and tips for sustainable outdoor living.

These picnic locations are strategically situated near notable natural landmarks, so while enjoying a relaxed meal, visitors can witness features like bubbling hot springs, enclosed views of distant mountains, or even catch a glimpse of roaming wildlife. Some designated areas are equipped with outdoor chalkboards and illustrated guides, encouraging impromptu lessons in natural history. Rangers sometimes conduct scheduled "picnic talks" during peak hours, where they mix storytelling with science. They might discuss the life cycle of local species, explain the significance of geological formations, or conduct mini-activities that engage children and adults alike.

This integration of dining and learning is particularly effective for families who wish to combine relaxation with enrichment. When surrounded by nature's serene backdrop, conversations naturally shift to observations of the environment—children might ask why certain trees are present while their parents ponder the rock formations beneath their feet. Such organic interactions deepen one's understanding and appreciation for the park, highlighting the importance of ecological balance and the interconnectedness of life. Moreover, many picnic spots are dotted with art installations created by local artists and educational exhibits that rotate seasonally, offering fresh perspectives each visit and continuously re-energizing the learning experience.

## Ranger-Led Tours: Exploring Yellowstone Through Expert Eyes

Interacting directly with park rangers is one of the most enriching ways to experience Yellowstone. The park's ranger-led tours are designed to offer detailed insights into the park's natural and cultural heritage, combined with firsthand observations of living ecological and geological processes. Ranger-led tours vary from short, focused walks around features like a geyser basin to comprehensive hikes that delve into the history and science behind the park's formation.

Rangers serve not only as storytellers but also as living textbooks, relating complex scientific concepts in relatable narratives. During these tours, participants learn why Yellowstone was the first national park, how volcanic activity shapes its unique landscapes, and what ongoing conservation efforts are being implemented to protect endangered habitats. Detailed explanations about the thermal dynamics of geysers, the behavior patterns of local wildlife, and insights into the historical use of the land by Native American tribes provide context that enriches every step of the journey.

These guided experiences emphasize interactive engagement. For instance, a ranger may pause at a thermal feature and invite the group to observe the subtle cues that indicate an upcoming eruption. They might encourage visitors to record their observations, ask questions, and share their interpretations of the natural phenomena they witness. Many tours include opportunities for up-close encounters in safe, controlled environments, like viewing a steaming hot spring from a designated boardwalk, or visiting a remote area to spot bison and elk. Equipment such as binoculars and portable field guides may be distributed, empowering participants to continue the exploration independently once the tour concludes.

Moreover, ranger-led tours are frequently adapted to different age groups and interests. Specialized tours focus on the geology of the park, while others might target bird-watching or mammal tracking. This versatility ensures that every member of the family, from enthusiastic kids to seasoned naturalists, finds a tour that resonates with their interests and knowledge level. As rangers weave historical anecdotes with state- of-the-art scientific understanding, the tours become a dynamic, interactive lesson in American natural heritage, reinforcing both the beauty and the fragility of Yellowstone's ecosystems.

## Interactive Visitor Centers and Educational Exhibits

Upon entering Yellowstone, many visitors begin their journey at one of the park's visitor centers. These centers are treasure troves of educational exhibits, interactive displays, and informative multimedia presentations that provide a comprehensive background to the park's natural wonders. Designed to be both engaging and easily accessible, the exhibits often include a mix of hands-on activities, digital installations, and traditional displays that highlight key aspects of Yellowstone's ecology and history.

Inside these centers, large-format maps, dioramas, and interactive touch screens offer in-depth information on how geological forces shaped the park over millennia. Detailed exhibits explain the science behind geothermal features, the sustainability practices in place to protect delicate ecosystems, and even the processes of wildlife migration and behavior. Visitors can explore interactive models that simulate volcanic eruptions or the unique ecology of thermal pools, gaining a visceral understanding of complex natural phenomena through visual and tactile engagement.

Families with children are particularly drawn to the centers' interactive areas. These spaces often feature puzzles, video displays, and games that challenge visitors to match animal tracks with species, decipher the code behind geyser intervals, or virtually reconstruct an ancient landscape using digital tools. This hands-on approach transforms the visitor center into a dynamic, educational playground where learning is achieved through discovery rather than passive absorption of facts. The integration of technology and tactile learning underlines the park's commitment to making science accessible and fun.

Guided tours of the visitor centers are available at regular intervals and are led by educational specialists or park rangers. These tours provide an opportunity to understand the narrative behind each exhibit, often relating academic information to the actual experiences waiting just outside the doors. Whether you are a first-time visitor or a returning guest, these centers provide a critical context, transforming abstract scientific theories into concrete and observable realities that you can witness as you explore the park.

## Family Exploration Challenges: Scavenger Hunts and Nature Trails

For families seeking an extra layer of adventure, Yellowstone offers a variety of exploration challenges designed to transform a simple hike into an engaging quest. One popular activity is the park-wide **scavenger hunt**, where participants are given a list of natural landmarks and features to locate. Each list is carefully curated to include a mix of well-known and lesser-known treasures—from specific rock formations and unique flora to intriguing signs of geothermal activity. With maps and clues provided at the visitor centers, families set out to uncover hidden gems along designated trails.

The scavenger hunts are designed with educational goals in mind. As participants search for items on their list, they learn to identify distinct geological formations and observe subtle differences in plant life. Informational plaques along the trails often correlate with clues in the scavenger hunt, deepening your understanding of the natural processes at work. The activity also introduces visitors to the principles of navigation and observation, as you learn to use landmarks to orient yourself, read subtle signs in the environment, and understand ecological relationships.

In many cases, scavenger hunts are integrated with digital apps tailored for Yellowstone visitors. These apps can provide additional multimedia content, such as videos or audio clips that elaborate on the significance of each item found. As children check off each item, their excitement builds not only from the thrill of the hunt but also from the knowledge gained along the way. These challenges promote healthy competition among family members and serve as an excellent bonding activity, inspiring multiple generations to work together and share discoveries.

Additionally, some nature trails are specially designed to include physical and mental challenges that encourage problem-solving. On these trails, maps detail checkpoints that require visitors to answer trivia questions or complete short, fun challenges related to the local ecosystem. These interactive trail markers might ask you to count a specific type of wildflower, find evidence of a particular animal species, or even listen carefully for the sound of a distant waterfall. This blend of physical exercise, vigilance, and learning transforms a simple walk into an adventure that educates while it entertains.

## Seasonal Workshops and Special Programs

Yellowstone's calendar is peppered with seasonal workshops and special programs that cater to a range of interests—from art and photography to ecology and geology. These programs provide focused, in-depth sessions often led by guest experts or park researchers who bring specialized knowledge to the forefront. Workshops may be scheduled during quieter periods to allow for an intimate learning environment, or during peak season to manage larger groups in an interactive, structured format.

One notable example is the seasonal "Weather in Yellowstone" workshop, where visitors learn about the dynamic climate patterns that influence the park's natural processes. Through hands-on experiments and interactive displays, participants explore why the park experiences rapid weather changes, the impact of these fluctuations on local wildlife, and how climate change might be affecting these delicate ecosystems. Other sessions may include art classes that encourage participants to paint or sketch the park's majestic landscapes, with instructors offering tips on capturing light, color, and form. Such workshops not only enhance visitors' appreciation of Yellowstone's beauty but also equip them with skills that can be applied long after they leave the park.

Special programs are often synchronized with natural events such as meteor showers, the blooming of wildflowers, or the migration of wildlife. These time-sensitive activities provide an opportunity to witness pivotal ecological events and understand their significance through the lens of science. Workshops focusing on the park's unique geothermal dynamics delve into the intricate science behind geyser eruptions and hot springs, often featuring live demonstrations and experiments that simulate natural processes using safe, controlled methods. Attendees walk away with a deeper, more nuanced understanding of the forces that shape Yellowstone's rugged terrain.

By participating in these programs, visitors not only gain knowledge but also contribute to ongoing citizen science projects. Some workshops encourage participants to record observations—whether it be temperature variations in different areas or behavioral patterns in local fauna—thus contributing valuable data to researchers monitoring the park's ecosystem. This active involvement fosters a sense of stewardship, as participants realize that their observations and learned insights can have a direct impact on conservation efforts and scientific understanding.

## Engaging with the Natural World: Environmental Education Activities

Yellowstone employs a range of environmental education activities that aim to bridge the gap between recreational enjoyment and scientific inquiry. Dedicated programs focus on topics such as wildlife conservation, sustainable practices, and the delicate balance of the park's ecosystems. These sessions are built on interactive discussions where park scientists and educators explain how everything in Yellowstone is interconnected—from the smallest insect to the largest mammal—and outline the ongoing efforts to preserve these natural relationships.

Workshops on wildlife biology often include live demonstrations and interactive displays, where attendees learn about tracking animal movements, understanding behavioral cues, and the role of each species in the larger ecological web. A hands-on session might involve examining replicas of animal prints and comparing them to tracks found in the wild, or using field guides to identify different species and understand their dietary habits. These experiences are designed to instill a deeper respect for all living creatures, emphasizing the importance of safeguarding biodiversity for future generations.

Environmental education in Yellowstone is also geared towards practical conservation. Sessions on sustainable outdoor practices highlight the importance of proper waste disposal, water conservation, and respecting designated trails to minimize human impact on sensitive habitats. Visitors learn about the "Leave No Trace" principles in an engaging and participatory manner. Interactive displays often challenge families to plan a "mini expedition" where they simulate managing resources and navigating ethical choices in a controlled environment. These activities not only educate but also motivate participants to implement environmentally responsible behaviours in their daily lives.

Collaborative projects are sometimes organized during longer visits or during special events. For instance, guided hikes may include a segment dedicated to collecting data on vegetation health or spotting signs of erosion, turning a routine walk into an impromptu research project. Rangers and educators provide the tools and training necessary for participants to gather useful environmental data. This hands-on involvement reinforces the idea that every visitor plays a role in managing and preserving the wonders of Yellowstone. As you help gather information, you also become an active participant in the park's ongoing conservation narrative.

## Exploring Through Technology: Mobile Apps and Digital Learning

Integrating modern technology with natural exploration, many visitors embrace Yellowstone's suite of digital tools that enhance the educational experience without distracting from the wonder of the outdoors. Dedicated mobile apps offer interactive maps replete with historical narratives, augmented reality features that bring geological phenomena to life, and live data feeds on current wildlife activity and weather conditions. Using these applications, you can embark on self-guided tours that incorporate quizzes, digital scavenger hunts, and informative pop-ups about the sites you visit.

The digital experience is designed to be intuitive and family-friendly. Interactive maps not only show trail routes and key features but also provide layers of information on plant species, wildlife hotspots, and even the optimal viewing spots for sunrise and sunset photography. Users can record their observations directly within the app, share photos with fellow park-goers on dedicated social networks, and even contribute their own discoveries to a growing online repository of Yellowstone experiences. The integration of technology thus reinforces learning by making scientific data, historical context, and conservation updates readily accessible through a device that many carry every day.

Parents appreciate the educational mobile apps as a means to engage even the most tech-savvy children with nature. Gamified learning challenges stimulate curiosity and reward exploration. For example, a family might set out with an app that challenges them to spot as many different bird species as possible, or to capture a series of photos that demonstrates the progression of sunlight across the park's terrain. In this way, outdoor exploration melds seamlessly with technology to create a dynamic learning journey that is both interactive and immersive.

## Celebrating the Natural Heritage: Art, Culture, and History Programs

A less conventional yet equally enriching aspect of Yellowstone's fun and educational activities is its focus on art and cultural expression. The park frequently hosts events that celebrate local art, storytelling, and the historical narratives of the region. These events foster a deeper connection between the cultural heritage of Yellowstone and its natural landscape. Workshops on nature-inspired art encourage visitors to use traditional media—such as watercolors, pastels, or sketching pencils—to capture the park's dramatic vistas, geothermal features, and wildlife portraits.

Local historians and Native American educators are often invited to share their perspectives on Yellowstone's rich heritage. Through storytelling sessions, you learn about the spiritual significance the land holds for indigenous communities, the historical usage of natural resources by early settlers, and the evolution of conservation efforts that led to the establishment of America's first national park. These programs provide context and meaning to the visual beauty that surrounds you, interweaving artistic expression with respect for history.

Sometimes, art exhibitions are paired with guided walks, where participants explore a particular aspect of the park while discussing themes such as change, resilience, and the passage of time. Outdoor galleries may feature temporary installations that use natural materials to highlight the contrast between human creativity and the ever- changing natural world. Educational panels provide insights into the inspiration behind these artworks, offering visitors a deeper understanding of how art can be both reflective and transformative. Such interdisciplinary approaches create a holistic

learning environment that celebrates the richness of Yellowstone's natural and cultural narrative.

## Engaging with Local Experts: Field Classes and Citizen Science

For visitors who wish to delve deeper into the science behind Yellowstone's phenomena, a selection of field classes and citizen science initiatives are available. These programs, often led by park researchers and local university experts, offer focused investigations on subjects ranging from wildlife behavior to geothermal chemistry. Participating in a field class means spending several hours immersed in an area, accompanied by experts ready to explain the intricate processes that govern the local ecosystem.

During these sessions, participants are given practical assignments such as observing animal tracks, sampling water from geothermal features (under strict safety guidelines), or recording ambient environmental data. These real-time experiments provide a window into the research methodologies used to monitor the park's health and ecological changes. Data collected by visitors can contribute to ongoing studies, making the experience both informative and impactful. Detailed field guides, safety equipment, and tutorials on basic scientific methods are provided before embarking on these classes, ensuring that participants of all ages and experience levels are prepared for an enriching experience in Yellowstone's diverse terrains.

Citizen science initiatives also include seasonal surveys where visitors help count bison, monitor vegetation changes, or track the emergence of wildflower blooms. The hands-on data collection fosters a genuine sense of responsibility and helps visitors understand that their observations can directly support conservation and management efforts. This active involvement not only enhances the educational value of your visit but also cultivates a collaborative spirit between park visitors and the scientific community. Educational talks given during these sessions provide context on how collected data influences management decisions and furthers our understanding of environmental dynamics.

## Combining Learning with Leisure: Tailored Family Itineraries

To maximize the educational value of your visit while keeping the experience fun and leisurely, Yellowstone offers tailored itineraries designed for families with different interests and age groups. These itineraries are carefully crafted to ensure a balance between active learning, physical exploration, and relaxation. For instance, a family itinerary might include a morning scavenger hunt on an easy nature trail, a mid-day interactive exhibit visit at a visitor center, and an evening stargazing session paired with a picnic dinner in one of the scenic recreation areas.

Each itinerary is mapped out with recommended stops that integrate educational moments naturally into your sightseeing experience. Detailed descriptions inform you about the historical significance of each landmark, the scientific stories behind geyser eruptions, and the cultural heritage embedded in the landscape. While you traverse established trails, the itinerary may suggest pauses at specific observation points where interpretive signs prompt reflections on natural cycles and conservation efforts. These planned stops ensure that the day is peppered with moments of both discovery and relaxation, making the experience enjoyable for children, teenagers, and adults alike.

Many itineraries also include optional interactive segments, such as timed nature quizzes or photo contests that encourage everyone to participate actively and share their discoveries. The design of these itineraries takes into account the various energy levels and interests within a family, ensuring that slower-paced activities are interspersed with more engaging, hands-on experiences. Families are encouraged to share feedback and observations during these journeys, with some programs offering follow-up sessions where participants can discuss their findings with a park ranger or educator. These reflective moments cement the learning experience and transform day-long adventures into rich, memory-filled narratives.

## Encouraging Lifelong Learning: Resources and Continuing Engagement

Yellowstone's fun and educational activities are just the beginning of a lifelong journey of learning and appreciation for the natural world. The park offers an array of resources—both purchasable and freely available—that allow visitors to carry their learning experience home. From well-curated guidebooks and field journals to online portals featuring video lectures, interactive maps, and downloadable educational materials, there is ample opportunity for continued engagement with Yellowstone's natural and cultural heritage.

After your visit, you might explore online communities of Yellowstone enthusiasts who share photographs, data observations, and personal stories, further enriching your understanding of the park's dynamic ecosystems. Many educational programs in the park encourage follow-up projects—such as creating your own nature journal or compiling a photo essay—that serve as personal tributes to the experience and extend the narrative of learning beyond the physical boundaries of Yellowstone. These resources help transform a single trip into an ongoing dialogue about conservation, scientific discovery, and the enduring beauty of our natural world.

The park's website and affiliated social media channels regularly update information on new educational initiatives, upcoming workshops, and citizen science projects. This continuous stream of content not only keeps the spirit of exploration alive but also invites former visitors to become active contributors to Yellowstone's legacy. Whether you are a parent looking for more ideas to nurture your child's interest in nature, or an individual inspired by the park's geological wonders, these resources provide a platform for both learning and sharing, fostering a global community united by a passion for the natural world.

## Bringing It Together: Practical Tips for Engaging Activities

To help you make the most of the fun and educational activities in Yellowstone, consider a few practical tips as you plan your adventure. First, carry a well-stocked field kit that includes a notebook, pencils, binoculars, and a camera or smartphone capable of both high-resolution images and short video clips. This kit will serve as your portable learning lab, allowing you to record observations, sketch details of unique rock formations, or capture the vivid colors of a geothermal pool.

Dress in layers and wear comfortable, sturdy footwear, as educational activities often involve a fair amount of walking and standing. Ensure that children are equipped with sun protection, hydration, and snacks—especially if they are expected to participate in a scavenger hunt or an extended ranger-led tour. Bring along printed maps or a downloaded copy of the park's digital guide to ensure that you remain oriented while exploring more remote areas.

Prior to your visit, review the schedule of ranger-led tours, workshops, and special events available during your travel dates. Reserving spots early can not only guarantee you partake in these educational experiences but also provide the opportunity to join groups with similar interests. Additionally, talk to park rangers or visitor center staff for personalized recommendations. They can advise on the best times of day for stargazing sessions, highlight emerging wildlife hotspots, or help you choose the most suitable Junior Ranger activities for your family's age group.

## Blueprints for a Memorable Experience

The array of fun and educational activities in Yellowstone stand as blueprints for a day filled with wonder, discovery, and personal growth. Each activity—from the structured learning of the Junior Ranger Program to the creative expression found in photography and journaling—offers layers of insight into the intricacies of our natural world. The park's emphasis on integrating education with recreation ensures that every visitor leaves not just with memories of breathtaking landscapes, but also with factual knowledge and a renewed sense of stewardship for nature.

Participating in ranger-led tours or joining seasonal workshops creates opportunities for intimate interactions with experts who are passionate about Yellowstone's legacy. The thoughtful blend of interactive visitor center exhibits, digital learning tools, and real-world explorations ensures that your journey is supported by both convenience and in-depth insights. The curated experiences motivate families to explore together, encouraging conversations that bridge generations and inspire future adventures.

While the physical beauty of Yellowstone is mesmerizing on its own, the educational components enrich your trip by delving into the scientific and cultural narratives behind every natural wonder. Interactive sessions, citizen science projects, and guided explorations transform each step into an opportunity to learn about evolutionary processes, chemical interactions in thermal features, or the conservation tactics that ensure the park's enduring vibrancy. Environmental education activities impart practical lessons in sustainable living and collective responsibility, reminding every visitor that their actions, as small as they may seem, contribute to the park's ongoing story.

Yellowstone remains a place where every element—whether it is a wandering stream, a towering tree, or a geyser's rhythmic eruption—serves as a lesson in natural artistry and scientific wonder. The fun and educational activities available within the park are thoughtfully arranged to ensure that your adventure is not only exhilarating but also deeply informative. By engaging in these activities, each visitor becomes an active participant in a grand narrative that celebrates the planet's geological history, vibrant ecosystems, and the enduring human spirit of exploration.

Planning your day with a mix of structured programs and spontaneous exploration ensures that you immerse yourself fully in the dynamic educational landscape of Yellowstone. Reflect on each interaction with nature as an invitation to rediscover the fundamentals of science, art, and culture—all seamlessly intertwined in an environment that has been captivating visitors for generations. As you capture stunning photographs, complete your Junior Ranger badge, stargaze under an expansive night sky, or join fellow explorers in a citizen science survey, you solidify a bond with this extraordinary place that transcends a single visit.

Whether you are a returning visitor eager to unravel more of Yellowstone's mysteries or a first-time guest stepping into an unparalleled classroom of nature, the fun and educational activities woven throughout the park transform each moment into a narrative of exploration, inspiration, and shared discovery. Plan to take a reflective walk along a nature trail, pause to marvel at geological wonders, or simply sit quietly at a picnic area while digesting the vast information laid out before you. In Yellowstone, learning is a continuous and immersive experience where every glance, every conversation, and every natural spectacle reinforces the profound interconnectedness of our world.

Yellowstone's commitment to environmental education, combined with its stunning landscapes and curated interactive programs, lays the groundwork for memories that will stay with you for a lifetime. From the joy of earning the Junior Ranger badge to the satisfaction of contributing to real scientific research, each activity in the park is intricately designed to educate and delight simultaneously. By engaging with these educational opportunities, you not only enhance your own understanding of the natural world but also join a community of nature enthusiasts dedicated to preserving the legacy of this iconic national park.

Armed with digital tools, field guides, and the insights provided by experienced rangers and educators, your journey into Yellowstone becomes more than a sightseeing trip—it becomes a comprehensive educational adventure. As you plan your route, participate in guided tours, and explore curated exhibits, every step transforms into a lesson in the grandeur of geological history and the subtle nuances of living ecosystems. This synthesis of learning and leisure establishes Yellowstone as a living classroom where nature teaches and every visitor becomes both a student and a steward of its heritage.

# NEARBY ATTRACTIONS & DAY TRIPS

## Exploring Beyond Yellowstone: Nearby Attractions & Day Trips

Yellowstone National Park is a treasure in itself, offering boundless wonders and adventures. Yet, for those with a bit more time or a spirit eager for variety, the surroundings of Yellowstone provide a unique extension of the experience. With destinations ranging from dramatic national parks to charming frontier towns that echo the Old West, visitors can immerse themselves in a broader slice of the American landscape. Whether you are cruising along scenic routes, exploring historical sites, or encountering small-town charm, the region adjacent to Yellowstone is brimming with attractions that enrich and complement your primary adventure.

## Grand Teton National Park: A Natural Masterpiece

Located just a short drive south of Yellowstone, Grand Teton National Park introduces visitors to a completely different but equally mesmerizing landscape. With its striking snow-capped peaks, pristine alpine lakes, and abundant wildlife, the park is a haven for photography enthusiasts, hikers, and nature lovers seeking a quieter retreat from Yellowstone's bustling geothermal marvels.

### Scenic Splendor and Iconic Views

Grand Teton National Park is renowned for its dramatic mountain vistas and clear, reflective lakes such as Jenny Lake and Jackson Lake. The towering Teton Range, whose rugged silhouette frames the horizon, serves as an unforgettable backdrop. Drive along the park's scenic byways to experience panoramic views at every turn. In spring and summer, wildflowers blanket the meadows while herds of elk graze in the open, making it the perfect time for nature photography and peaceful contemplation.

The park's main roadway provides stops at several noteworthy viewpoints. At Oxbow Bend, you'll catch a glimpse of the Tetons perfectly mirrored in the Snake River—a subtle reminder of nature's artistry. Meanwhile, Signal Mountain Lodge offers several observation decks for those eager to appreciate the mountain panorama while taking a leisurely break with a cup of hot coffee.

### Outdoor Activities and Adventures

For visitors keen on outdoor pursuits, Grand Teton National Park is a veritable playground. Hiking trails crisscross the park, ranging from gentle nature walks to demanding backcountry treks. The Cascade Canyon Trail is a popular option for families and seasoned hikers alike, offering a blend of wildflower meadows, serene river views, and the chance to observe a robust array of wildlife. More adventurous travelers can explore the rugged terrain leading to Icefall Canyon, where glaciers slowly shape the landscape and provide insight into the geological processes that formed the Tetons.

Water enthusiasts are drawn to Jenny Lake, not only for its beauty but also for the assortment of water sports. Canoeing or kayaking on its still waters gives a new dimension to appreciation of the surrounding cliffs and forests. For those interested in learning more about the natural history of the area, guided boat tours are available, offering insights into the interconnected ecosystems of the region.

### Wildlife and Conservation Encounters

Much like Yellowstone, Grand Teton National Park is a sanctuary for wildlife. Early morning and late afternoon are ideal times to observe the park's inhabitants, including bison, moose, and black bears. Guides and park rangers often provide interpretation sessions that enhance your understanding of these creatures' habits and the importance of preserving their habitats. This proximity to nature's raw beauty and abundant species serves as both an exhilarating experience and a poignant reminder of conservation priorities in America's national parks.

### Accommodations and Visitor Services

The park is well-equipped with a range of visitor facilities. From rustic lodges nestled in the natural environment to well-appointed visitor centers where you can gather trail maps and local information, Grand Teton caters to every taste and level of adventure. During peak seasons, it is wise to reserve accommodations well in advance. For those seeking a more immersive experience, campsites are available that offer the opportunity to sleep under the same stars that have inspired generations of artists and naturalists. With interpretive programs and ranger-led excursions, every visit promises opportunities for education mixed with outdoor recreation.

### Suggested Itinerary for a Day Trip

For those with limited time, a day trip to Grand Teton National Park can be thoroughly rewarding. Begin with an early morning drive to Oxbow Bend to witness the sunrise over the Snake River. Follow up with a leisurely breakfast at one of the park's lodges before setting out on a hike around Jenny Lake. In the afternoon, consider a guided boat tour to gain a deeper understanding of the park's geological and ecological narrative. Wrap up your day with a scenic drive along the park's backroads, stopping at various overlooks until nighttime descends, and the monumental Tetons are silhouetted against the setting sun.

## Cody, Wyoming: Stepping Back in Time

Head east from Yellowstone and you'll find the vibrant town of Cody, Wyoming, a place where the spirit of the Old West is preserved and celebrated. Named after the legendary showman William F. "Buffalo Bill" Cody, this town offers a stark yet charming contrast to the pristine wilderness of Yellowstone, inviting visitors to explore its historical significance and enjoy a blend of cultural attractions and modern amenities.

### Western Heritage and Cultural Attractions

Cody's rich historical tapestry is interwoven with tales of rugged frontiers and pioneering adventures. The centerpiece is the Buffalo Bill Center of the West, an expansive complex of five museums that cover a broad spectrum of subjects, including American Indian history, the natural history of the region, and the legacy of Buffalo Bill himself. Here, interactive exhibits, restored artifacts, and detailed narratives bring the vibrant history of the American West to life.

Walking through the downtown area, you will encounter historic buildings that once served as saloons, general stores, and boarding houses. A visit to Cody's Frontier Days arena is a must during the summer months when the city hosts one of the largest outdoor rodeos in the country. This event not only pits the skills of cowboys in rodeo events but also celebrates the traditions and community spirit that have defined this part of Wyoming for over a century.

### Unique Experiences and Outdoor Recreation

Beyond its historical attractions, Cody also offers plenty for those who prefer the outdoors. The nearby Shoshone National Forest, which stretches east of the town, presents a wealth of recreational opportunities such as hiking, fishing, and horseback riding. In the crisp mountain air, adventure seekers can traverse trails that meander through dense forests and alpine meadows, each step echoing the footsteps of pioneers who once roamed these lands.

For those interested in a glimpse of wildlife in a more controlled setting, local ranches offer horseback riding tours that combine the thrill of the Wild West with the comfort of a guided experience. These tours often include educational narratives about the local ecosystem, Native American lore, and the adventurous life of cowboys. Whether you ride along the rugged trails or simply enjoy a scenic picnic on a ranch, Cody seamlessly blends nature with culture.

### Local Culinary Delights and Hospitality

Cody's warm and inviting atmosphere is mirrored in its culinary offerings. Several local eateries serve a mix of hearty Western fare and modern American cuisine. Dine on bison burgers, fresh trout, and locally sourced produce in establishments that often feature regional décor and live music. The town's hospitable spirit extends to its accommodation options as well—from historic bed-and-breakfasts that evoke the charm of yesteryear to contemporary hotels equipped with modern conveniences. Each lodging option is designed to provide a comfortable and culturally immersive experience after a day of exploration.

### Practical Tips for Visiting Cody

When planning your trip to Cody, consider the seasonal events that might enrich your experience. Summer in Cody is synonymous with festivals, rodeos, and cultural exhibitions, while winter transforms the town into a quieter haven for those who enjoy snow sports and a nostalgic, old-time atmosphere. Visitors are encouraged to check local calendars for events such as Cody Stampede Rides and the annual Frontier Days celebration; these events can add a vibrant layer to your itinerary.

A well-planned day trip from Yellowstone to Cody is easily manageable. The drive itself is a scenic journey through the high country of Wyoming, with ample opportunities to stop along the road for photographs or brief hikes. Travel guides and local visitor centers provide updated maps and insights, ensuring that your journey is both safe and memorable.

## Jackson Hole: The Gateway to the West

Nestled in the spectacular Jackson Hole valley, the town of Jackson, Wyoming, offers both natural beauty and cultural sophistication. As a vibrant hub that attracts artists, adventurers, and discerning travelers alike, Jackson combines the outdoor excitement of the surrounding wilderness with the urban comforts of a cosmopolitan village.

### The Charismatic Town of Jackson

Jackson is instantly recognizable by its iconic antler arches that frame the town square —an enduring symbol of its vibrant cowboy spirit and celebration of its frontier past. The town's streets are lined with authentic Western architecture, upscale boutiques, art galleries, and gourmet dining options, making it an inviting destination for those looking to balance raw adventure with refined leisure.

A stroll through Jackson's historic downtown reveals local craft shops where artisans sell handcrafted leather goods, jewelry, and unique souvenirs that celebrate the wild spirit of the West. For art enthusiasts, several galleries and cultural centers host rotating exhibits that capture the essence of the landscapes and lifestyles in the region. Additionally, local cafes and bistros offer a taste of modern culinary trends infused with regional ingredients, ensuring that every meal is as memorable as the views.

### Outdoor Adventures Abound

Jackson's location at the foothills of the Teton Range makes it an excellent base for a variety of outdoor activities. In the winter months, the nearby Jackson Hole Mountain Resort becomes a playground for skiers and snowboarders, featuring challenging slopes and breathtaking alpine scenery. The town's close proximity to national parks and wilderness areas also presents ideal conditions for summer adventures—hiking, mountain biking, fly fishing, and wildlife safaris are commonplace.

For those on a more leisurely pursuit, a ride on one of the local scenic chairlifts or aerial tramways offers a gentle way to experience soaring views of the valley below. Alternatively, consider an evening wildlife tour, where experienced guides help locate and observe elk, moose, and even the elusive mountain goat against the backdrop of a twilight sky. These excursions offer a striking contrast to the geothermal wonders of Yellowstone, emphasizing the diversity of the region's natural beauty.

### Local Festivals and Cultural Offerings

Jackson is not only a gateway for outdoor enthusiasts but also a lively center for cultural events. Throughout the year, the town hosts festivals and performances that celebrate its artistic roots and community spirit. The Jackson Hole Fall Arts Festival, for example, draws painters, sculptors, and photographers from across the nation, all eager to capture the beauty of the high country. Meanwhile, local theaters and performance venues showcase live music, regional dance, and storytelling sessions that highlight the rich oral traditions of the American West.

The town also serves as a gateway to indigenous history, with opportunities to learn about the traditions and history of Native American tribes that once thrived in the valley. Museums and dedicated cultural centers offer guided tours that explain the significance of local motifs, weaving together stories of survival, resilience, and cultural resurgence.

### Crafting the Perfect Day Trip to Jackson

A day trip to Jackson from Yellowstone is an ideal blend of urban exploration and outdoor adventure. Start your morning with a hearty breakfast in one of Jackson's renowned cafés, where locally roasted coffee and fresh pastries energize you for the day ahead. Follow this with a brisk drive over scenic mountain passes that reveal unexpected vistas at every bend. Once in town, spend your time exploring historical sites, shopping for unique souvenirs, and, if time permits, joining a guided nature walk that introduces you to the local flora and fauna. In the late afternoon, consider a relaxing visit to one of the local spas or winery tastings, where you can savor the region's artisanal products before concluding your excursion.

## Scenic Routes and Additional Day Trips

While Grand Teton, Cody, and Jackson provide some of the most high-profile destinations, the region surrounding Yellowstone is peppered with lesser-known routes and stops that equally deserve attention. These scenic byways offer travelers a chance to break away from the main attractions and discover hidden gems that capture the essence of the American West.

## The Beartooth Highway: An Epic Road Trip

A drive along the Beartooth Highway is often described as one of America's most spectacular road trips. Winding through the Absaroka-Beartooth Wilderness, this route features steep mountain passes, sweeping valleys, and crystalline alpine lakes that present a dramatic contrast to the geothermal features of Yellowstone. With numerous pullouts and picnic areas, the highway invites travelers to stop frequently, breathe in the crisp mountain air, and appreciate nature's grandeur. During the summer months, the road is lined with wildflowers and buzzing with life, while in early autumn, the foliage shifts to a tapestry of reds, oranges, and yellows—an unforgettable visual feast.

Planning your Beartooth Highway adventure requires a bit of preparation. Check road conditions and seasonal closures as weather in these high-altitude areas can change rapidly. Bring along a detailed map, plenty of water, and layers to adjust to temperature fluctuations. As you embark on this drive, be sure to allocate extra time for spontaneous stops—each turn may reveal secret waterfalls, historic markers, or friendly local diners where you can sample a slice of regional cuisine.

## West Yellowstone and Surrounding Areas

Just outside Yellowstone's north entrance, the town of West Yellowstone offers another convenient and enjoyable day trip destination. Known for its family-friendly atmosphere and local charm, this town is a wonderful gateway to additional outdoor activities. In West Yellowstone, visitors can take advantage of cross-country skiing in winter, mountain biking and hiking in summer, and even snowmobiling during transitional seasons. Local museums and visitor centers often feature exhibits that delve into the early history of Yellowstone's establishment, providing context that enriches your overall park experience.

Guided tours and recreational outfitters in West Yellowstone offer a variety of day trips, from rafting adventures on nearby rivers to wildlife photography tours in less- traveled areas. Whether you choose a guided excursion or decide to explore on your own, West Yellowstone's proximity to the park ensures you continue to experience the natural splendor that defines the region.

## Cultural and Historical Detours

For those looking to combine outdoor beauty with cultural insights, several smaller towns dot the region with fascinating stories and vibrant traditions. Consider a visit to Red Lodge, Montana, where the spirit of the pioneer era is still celebrated through local festivals, antique shops, and museums that recount the tales of early settlers. In this town, local guides are often more than happy to share personal anecdotes about the landscape's historical significance and the ways in which the wilderness shaped community life.

Another enriching stop is Cooke City, located near the eastern entrance of Yellowstone. This quaint mountain village offers a glimpse into frontline wilderness life, where time-honored customs have been preserved. Explore small local galleries showcasing regional art, stop by family-run diners serving hearty mountain breakfasts, or simply take a leisurely walk around town as you discover remnants of a bygone era. These cultural detours provide context to the rich tapestry of life surrounding Yellowstone and allow for an immersive experience far removed from the more frequently visited tourist paths.

## Planning Your Multi-Destination Itinerary

When planning day trips and scenic drives around Yellowstone, it is essential to integrate flexibility into your itinerary. Each destination—be it Grand Teton's rugged elegance, Cody's vibrant historical charm, or Jackson's artistic allure—offers its own rhythm and pace. Use your time wisely by balancing planned excursions with opportunities to follow local recommendations. Visitor centers, local guides, and community bulletin boards are invaluable resources for discovering seasonal events, temporary exhibits, or last-minute festivals that might perfectly complement your trip.

For families, consider designing an itinerary that includes both natural pursuits and cultural experiences. Start with a morning exploration of a national park, alternating with a midday cultural visit in a nearby town. This dynamic approach can keep children engaged and allow parents to appreciate the broader historical and natural contexts of the region. Many local attractions provide interactive exhibits, hands-on activities, and guided tours geared specifically toward younger audiences, ensuring that even the smallest travelers have a meaningful and educational visit.

## Practical Considerations for Extended Excursions

A successful journey beyond Yellowstone hinges on a few key practical considerations. First, ensure that your vehicle is well-prepared for mountain roads and potential high-altitude conditions. Whether you're navigating the twisting turns of the Beartooth Highway or straying off the beaten path to visit Red Lodge, proper maintenance and a thorough pre-trip check of fluids, tires, and brakes are essential.

Second, plan for fluctuating weather conditions. Even during summer, mornings and evenings in the mountains can be brisk. Pack versatile layers, ranging from moisture- wicking shirts to insulated jackets. Rain gear, sturdy hiking boots, and extra food and water supplies are also advisable, especially if you embark on trails or less-traveled routes.

Third, stay informed about local conditions by checking weather websites and local news updates. Some remote areas may have limited cell service, so carrying a printed map along with a charged power bank can prove invaluable. Familiarize yourself with local emergency services and park ranger contacts, ensuring that you're prepared for any eventuality.

## Integrating Local Flavors and Community Engagement

One of the great joys of exploring the regions around Yellowstone is engaging with people who have a deep connection to the landscape. In towns like Cody and Jackson, local residents are often eager to share stories about their community's history, cultural traditions, and favorite outdoor spots. A conversation over a meal in a rustic diner or a visit to a local store can yield recommendations that no travel guide can fully capture. Whether it's the secret best time to view wildlife from a certain overlook, or the perfect local restaurant featuring regional specialties, these interactions add a personal touch that can transform your journey into an authentic experience.

Consider setting aside time to participate in community events, even if they are small and seemingly off the radar. Local farmers' markets, historical reenactments, and art fairs provide insights into the traditions and values that have shaped the region's identity. These cultural engagements also offer a chance to bring home not just souvenirs, but memories enriched by the warmth of local hospitality.

## Exploring at Your Own Pace

Every traveler's ideal journey is unique. Some may choose to plan every minute of their day, while others might prefer spontaneous adventures guided by local recommendations. The region surrounding Yellowstone is remarkably accommodating to both styles. Visitors who relish detailed itineraries will find that maps, guidebooks, and park ranger recommendations can provide a solid framework for exploring the best that the area has to offer. Meanwhile, those with a more free- spirited approach can simply use these resources as pointers—allowing curiosity and the serendipity of the open road to determine each next stop.

For example, a traveler might begin their day with a structured visit to Grand Teton National Park, following a pre-planned hiking route that covers the most scenic lookout points. Following lunch, they could venture into a less-characterized area such as a local art gallery or a historical monument in a small town along the route to Cody. An evening drive through Jackson may lead to an impromptu stop at a roadside diner known only to locals. This blend of planning and spontaneity can make your multi-destination itinerary even more enriching.

## Embracing the Journey Between Destinations

While it is natural to focus on the landmark destinations, the journey itself between these attractions is equally important. Long stretches on mountain highways can be interjected with detours that lead to surprising vistas, secret picnic spots, and opportunities for reflection. The roads in this part of Wyoming and Montana are not just conduits to your next destination—they are part of the experience. Rolling hills, winding rivers, and intermittent signs of wildlife along the roadside create a narrative of discovery that compliments your main attractions.

For those interested in detailed route planning, consider piecing together segments of the journey with historical context. Many of the highways follow routes once traveled by Native American tribes, early settlers, and pioneers. Stopping at roadside markers that detail these historical narratives provides an added dimension to your journey, linking the natural beauty of the landscape with the echo of human endeavor that has defined this region for centuries.

## Local Festivals and Seasonal Celebrations

Different times of the year bring different flavors to the region. During the summer months, outdoor festivals are common, often featuring local music, crafts, and authentic regional cuisine. In Cody, for instance, summer events often showcase rodeos, outdoor concerts, and cultural exhibits that celebrate the town's cowboy heritage. Jackson, on the other hand, transforms into a bustling arts and cultural center during its Fall Arts Festival, where visitors can interact with artists and view contemporary interpretations of classic Western scenes.

Seasonal celebrations also extend to winter, when towns gear up for snow festivals that include ice sculpting competitions, winter rodeos, and community snowshoe excursions. Such events not only provide entertainment during the colder months but also reflect a resilience and adaptability that is integral to life in the high country. Checking local calendars and planning your trip around these events can add an extra layer of excitement to your multi-destination itinerary.

## Savoring the Landscape and Its Stories

The collective experience of visiting areas surrounding Yellowstone is one steeped in both natural grandeur and historical nuance. Imagine watching the sunrise over the Tetons, with each ray illuminating a different chapter of geological history, then shifting gears to listen to the tale of Buffalo Bill's frontier exploits in Cody. Later, as you traverse the lively streets of Jackson, you absorb both the contemporary cultural pulse and echoes of centuries past. Each stop is a chapter in an ongoing narrative of the American West—a narrative that continues to evolve with every visitor's journey.

Throughout your travels, local guides often emphasize that the most rewarding experiences come not just from reaching a destination but from engaging deeply with each location's story. Whether you join a ranger-led discussion in a national park, chat with a local artist in a quaint workshop, or participate in a community celebration, you are witnessing firsthand the intricate interplay between history, nature, and culture that defines this vibrant corner of America.

## Planning to Return

Given the wealth of experiences available, consider planning for multiple trips if time permits. One journey might focus on the natural wonders of Yellowstone and Grand Teton, while another could concentrate on the cultural and historical insights offered by Cody, Jackson, and the smaller detour towns. Each visit provides a new perspective—the seasons transform landscapes, and evolving local events present opportunities to experience the region in fresh, delightful ways.

When planning subsequent trips, keep a travel journal or log, noting favorite stops, unexpected discoveries, and personal encounters. This record not only helps in refining future itineraries, but also creates a living document of your evolving relationship with the land. Many long-time travelers find that each return visit deepens their appreciation of the place and its stories, turning an initial adventure into a lifelong journey of discovery.

## Essential Tips for a Multi-Faceted Trip

No comprehensive trip is complete without practical tips that enhance both the travel experience and personal safety. Here are a few key recommendations as you venture into the diverse attractions around Yellowstone:

- **Vehicle Readiness:** Ensure your vehicle is well-maintained and equipped with essentials—spare tires, emergency kits, extra water, and a detailed paper map along with a reliable GPS device. Mountain routes and remote stretches may not have readily available services, so preparation is key.

- **Timing Your Visits:** Many attractions have distinct peak times. Plan early morning visits for wildlife sightings and the quiet moments of nature before the crowds arrive. Mornings often provide the soft light that is best for photography as well.

- **Local Insight:** Engage with local visitor centers as soon as you arrive at each destination. They provide up-to-date information on road conditions, seasonal events, and even off-the-beaten-path recommendations that may not appear in mainstream guidebooks.

- **Seasonal Adaptation:** The climate in high-altitude areas can be unpredictable. Always have weather-appropriate clothing, and check forecasts before heading out. Keeping layers on hand ensures that you can adapt to the cool mornings, warm afternoons, and eventual chills as the day winds down.

- **Cultural Sensitivity:** While exploring cultural sites and small towns, remember that you are stepping into communities with deep-rooted traditions. Respect local customs and support community-run establishments, which not only enrich your experience but also contribute positively to the local economy.

- **Flexible Itinerary:** Allow ample time between destinations so that travel is not rushed. Opportunities for spontaneous detours often lead to the most memorable surprises—a roadside café with homemade pies, a hidden viewpoint known only to locals, or an impromptu encounter with wildlife along a quiet country road.

## A Mosaic of Memories

The region surrounding Yellowstone is extraordinary in its diversity. Each destination —from Grand Teton's pristine alpine landscapes and Cody's storied frontier legacy to Jackson's blend of cultural sophistication and rugged outdoor adventure—contributes its own chapter to the larger narrative of the American West. Embracing these opportunities through well-planned day trips and scenic drives transforms your trip into a mosaic of memories, each piece enriched by history, nature, and heartfelt local engagement.

As you set out on these adventures, keep an open mind and a spirit of exploration. Whether capturing the fleeting moment of wildlife in a sun-dappled meadow, listening to the echoes of the past in a historic frontier town, or simply relishing the scenic serenity from the windows of your car along winding mountain roads, you are participating in a dynamic dialogue between nature and culture that continues to inspire and inform all who experience it.

Each drive, each conversation with locals, and each midday pause in a sunlit clearing becomes part of an ongoing journey that not only enriches your understanding of Yellowstone but also deepens your connection to this vast wilderness and its storied neighbors. The memories you create on these day trips will linger long after you leave, offering a renewed sense of wonder every time you recall the majestic Tetons, the rustic charm of Cody, and the vibrant heartbeat of Jackson.

Traveling in these regions is about more than visiting points on a map—it is about immersing yourself in environments that have defined American adventure for generations. The scenic routes, cultural stops, and spontaneous encounters outside of Yellowstone offer a full-bodied experience where nature's grandeur and human narratives intertwine seamlessly. In every turn of the road, every shared smile in a small town, and every moment of awe in the great outdoors, you add your own story to this remarkable landscape.

Carrying practical advice, local insights, and a genuine curiosity about the heritage of the area, this extended journey ensures that every day spent beyond the confines of Yellowstone continues to be an adventure as enriching and transformative as the park itself. Take advantage of the variety of attractions and experiences available, planned in a way that balances exploration and relaxation. In this way, each day trip not only complements your Yellowstone adventure but also stands on its own as a testament to the diverse and captivating spirit of the American West.

Made in the USA
Coppell, TX
29 June 2025